An Outline History of
Classical Chinese Literature

中國古典文學史大綱
馮沅君著
楊憲益、戴乃迭譯

An Outline History of Classical Chinese Literature

by Feng Yuanjun
translated by Yang Xianyi
and Gladys Yang

Joint Publishing Co.
Hongkong 1983

Joint Publishing Co. (HK)
9 Queen Victoria St., Hongkong

© Joint Publishing Co. (HK) 1983

First published October 1983

Printed in Hongkong by
Bright Sun Printing Press Co., Ltd.
5/F., Blk. B, 17 Yuk Yat St., Kowloon, Hong Kong.

ISBN 962.04.0227.8

Publisher's Note

This book outlines the history of Chinese literature from its genesis to the May Fourth Movement of 1919, which marks the birth of modern Chinese literature.

Originally entitled *A Short History of Classical Chinese Literature*, it was first published in 1958 by Foreign Languages Press, Beijing. In this new edition we have converted the transcription of Chinese characters into Hanyu pinyin and made some minor changes where appropriate.

Contents

I. The Origin of Chinese Literature

The primitive men who were our ancestors could not even speak at first; but to work together they had to convey their ideas, and so gradually they learned to utter complex sounds. Suppose they were carrying logs and found it hard work, but did not know how to express this; if one of them called out "Yo, heave, ho!" that was a literary creation. And if others, admiring him, took it up, this was a form of publication. If it were recorded by some method it would become literature, and of course such a man would be an author or writer of the Yo-heave-ho school. . . . Today we still have folk songs, ballads, fishermen's chants and the like everywhere, which are also the work of illiterate poets. Then there are folk tales, which are stories by illiterate writers. So all these men are illiterate men of letters.*

Lu Xun points out in the above passage that the earliest authors were the labouring people, who composed the first — unwritten — literature during the course of their work.

---

* Lu Xun, "A Layman's Remarks on Writing", collected in *Essays of Qiejieting*, 1934. The present English translations are quoted from *Lu Xun: Selected Works*, Vol. IV (Beijing: Foreign Languages Press, 1980), translated by Yang Xianyi and Gladys Yang.

To lighten the burden of their toil and express the joy of achievement, the ancient Chinese, like the first men in every country, created rhythmic sounds and language which became the earliest poetry; while, as the centuries went by, labour heightened their perceptive powers and their aesthetic sense developed.

In the early vernacular literature, myths and legends had a special significance.

As the life of primitive men was hard and their knowledge was limited, they had no scientific explanation for natural or social phenomena: heaven and earth, the sun and the moon, mountains and rivers, wind and rain, thunder and lightning, birds, beasts and plants, the origin of human life, the invention of tools, or men's struggle for a happier existence. Instead they tried to understand and explain these things on the basis of their own experience, thus creating many beautiful myths and legends.

The story of the flood is a case in point. This myth is widely known, different versions existing in different parts of China. But the best known of all the heroes alleged to have pacified the flood is Yu the Great.

Yu's father, Gun, undertook the arduous task of curbing the flood. He consulted two wise creatures that lived in the water and constructed dykes to prevent inundations, but the flood only became worse until Heaven grew angry and killed him, and his corpse was left three years without burial. In these three years, however, his body remained unrotted and Yu was born from it to go on with his work. Yu struggled against many monsters and evil spirits who obstructed him; he raised great earthworks to stop the flood's advance and cut channels to let it pass. After toiling for eight years, he finally pacified the flood and enabled the people to live in peace and happiness.

This myth tells of the courage and perseverance of our ancestors in their battle with nature, and how undaunted they were by death and difficulties — when one fell another stepped into his place. Though this myth may strike modern readers as fantastic, it reflects men's determination to build themselves a better life. Stories with a deep significance like this can educate successive generations and become a force to impel society forward. They remain, too, an inspiration for later writers, leaving their mark on the nation's poetry, fiction and drama.

Early Chinese literature was also rich in songs and riddles, but after the lapse of so many centuries the majority of these are lost, while some were so modified when recorded by later scribes that we no longer know their original form.

As mankind advanced, a written language was invented. In China a distinctive ideographic script was developed, starting with pictographs or simplified drawings, such as 𛰫 for man, 𛰬 for bird, 𛰭 for moon, or 𛰮 for mountain. Gradually these pictograms became stylized, and indirect symbols, associate compounds, phonetic loan words and other types of characters were added. The special nature of the Chinese language, which is remarkably laconic and evocative if sometimes ambiguous, has helped to give classical Chinese literature certain of its distinctive features: succinctness and vigour. And relatively few changes have taken place in the written language over the last three thousand years.

Of the earliest writings extant, some are genuine and some are spurious. In other words, there are records attributed to the Xia and Shang dynasties, or even to the time of the three sage emperors, which were actually written during or after the Zhou dynasty, perhaps based on earlier materials. The earliest genuine writings are the oracles of the Shang dynasty inscribed on the shoulder-blades of mammals or the shells of turtles. The answers of the gods to various questions were indicated by the shape of the cracks produced when the bones were heated, and inscriptions on the bones recorded the results. Records of important events were also inscribed on bronze vessels.

By the Shang dynasty China had a slave society. Agriculture, husbandary and handicrafts were already comparatively developed, and on this basis a strong state of slaves and slave-owners was established with a fairly high level

4

Oracle bone recording scantiness of rain,
Shang Dynasty

of civilization.

The inscriptions on oracle bones and bronze vessels are usually short, though certain bronze inscriptions number more than thirty words and some of those on oracle bones more than a hundred. In the main these recorded the activities of the rulers, but they also reflect conditions of work at that time. Since these records are mostly in prose, we can consider them as our earliest prose literature. Some, however, resemble songs, as in the following case:

We ask the oracle on gui si *day:*
Is there going to be any rain?
Rain from the east?

Rain from the west?
Rain from the north?
Rain from the south?

This seems to be an incantation for rain, reflecting those early husbandmen's desire for a bountiful harvest.

Most of these ancient incantations in prose and verse date from before the eleventh century B.C. This can be considered as the beginning of Chinese literature, the first chapter in our classical literature.

II. Zhou Dynasty Literature

1. Western Zhou, Spring and Autumn Period

By the eleventh century B.C., King Wu of Zhou had destroyed the Shang dynasty and the slave-owning form of society was beginning to distintegrate. A feudal society was gradually evolved which persisted for several thousand years. The second period in the history of classical Chinese literature is the eight hundred years from the founding of the Western Zhou dynasty to the end of the third century B.C. when the First Emperor of Qin, also known as Qin Shi Huang Di, united all China.

Let us first look at early Zhou literature, for after the Spring and Autumn Period some important changes took place. The masterpieces of this age are *The Book of Songs*, and certain sections of *The Book of History* as well as of *The Book of Change.*

The *Book of Songs* is the earliest anthology of poetry in China and one of her greatest treasures. It contains more than three hundred songs composed before the sixth century B.C., most of them with four characters to a line. Some are ancient songs for dances and sacrifices, others narrative poetry and satire belonging to a later period, yet others folk-songs from different districts, reflecting the life and thoughts of the common people.

Like the early poetry of other countries, most of these

songs were associated with dances representing different forms of work or fertility rites. The section called "Hymns of Zhou " in *The Book of Songs* includes several poems dealing with agriculture, the best of these being "They Clear Away the Grass, the Trees," and "Very Sharp, the Good Shares." These are probably folk-songs which were taken over by the rulers as sacrificial odes and may well have been changed or distorted in the process, for certain lines appear not altogether consistent. They conjure up for us a vivid picture of how the early Chinese serfs wrested a living from the soil three thousand years ago in the Yellow River Valley.

The ancients enjoyed narrative poems about the heroic deeds of their predecessors, and such poems can also be found in *The Book of Songs.* Some praise ancestors of the royal house, while others describe the exploits of earlier heroes or the resistance to invading northern tribes. Ancient Chinese literature has no great epic, yet from these narrative poems we can see how the Zhou people worked, administered the land and fought.

There are numerous satires too in this anthology. Though the husbandmen toiled hard and often went hungry and cold, they had to pay heavy taxes and levies, and also give free conscript labour or serve as soldiers. Some of the songs therefore criticize social injustice, contrasting the carefree and extravagant life of the rulers with the labourers' hard lot.

But the most important section of *The Book of Songs* is that comprising folk-songs of different localities. As the rulers collected these for their own purposes, certain alterations were inevitably made; yet even so these lyrics remain perennially lovely. "In the Seventh Month," which describes the occupations belonging to different seasons of the year, gives us an authentic glimpse of country life in autumn and winter:

> *In the ninth month we make ready the stackyards,*
> *In the tenth month we bring in the harvest,*
> *Millet for wine, millet for cooking, the early and the late,*

Paddy and hemp, beans and wheat.
Come, my husbandmen,
My harvesting is over,
Go up and begin your work in the house,
In the morning gather thatch-reeds,
In the evening twist rope;
Go quickly on to the roofs.
*Soon you will be beginning to sow your many grains.**

The serfs not only worked, hard for the lord of the manor, but endured humiliating treatment too — especially the womenfolk:

The spring days are drawing out;
They gather the white aster in crowds.
A girl's heart is sick and sad,
Forced to go home with the lord.

Hatred for their masters is expressed in such songs as "Chop, Chop, They Cut the Hardwood.":

You do not sow, you do not reap,
Yet you have corn, three hundred stackyards!
You do not hunt, you do not chase,
Yet see all those badgers hanging in your courtyard!

The poem"Great Rats, Great Rats" voices similar resentment and the longing for a better future:

Great rats, great rats,
Keep away from our wheat!
Three years we have worked for you,
But you have spurned us;
Now we shall leave this land
For a happier one —

* From *The Book of Songs*, translated by Arthur Waley.

That happy land, that happy land,
*There we shall find all that we need.**

There are many beautiful love poems in *The Book of Songs*. Some describe honest courtship and lasting devotion, others unhappy love affairs and marriages, and the sorrows peculiar to women in feudal times. Thus in the poem "We Thought You Were a Simple Peasant," at first we find two lovers devoted to each other.

I climbed that high wall
To catch a glimpse of Fu-kuan,
And when I could not see Fu-kuan,
My tears fell on the flood.
At last I caught sight of Fu-kuan,
And how gaily I laughed and talked!
You consulted your yarrow-stalks
And their patterns showed nothing unlucky.
You came with your cart
And moved me and my dowry.

But later the man proved untrue.

The mulberry leaves have fallen,
All yellow and seared,
Since I came to you,
Three years I have eaten poverty.
The waters of the Chi were in flood;
They wetted the curtains of the carriage.
It was not I who was at fault;
It is you who have altered your ways,
It is you who are unfaithful,
*Whose favours are cast this way and that.***

---

* From *The People Speak Out*, translated by Rewi Alley.
**From *The Book of Songs*, translated by Arthur Waley.

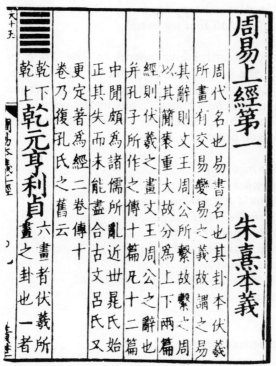

1265 edition of The Book of Change

The *Book of Songs*, especially its section of folk-songs, holds a very high position in Chinese literature. Though feudal commentators distorted the meaning of many of the poems, for over two thousand years this collection has been dear to innumerable Chinese readers. These beautiful lyrics with their graphic images and simple, evocative language give a true picture of life in the Zhou dynasty and laid the foundations of the fine tradition of realism in Chinese poetry.

Roughly contemporaneous with *The Book of Songs* are the historical records in *The Book of History* and the explanations of hexagrams used for divination in *The Book of Change.*

As Zhou dynasty prose developed from the Shang oracle bones and bronze inscriptions, *The Book of History* shows resemblances to the bronze inscriptions while *The Book of Change* is reminiscent of the earlier oracles. Much of *The Book of History* dates from a later period, but a few of the sections on the Western Zhou and early Eastern Zhou period were actually written at this time. Although most of these record the statements and actions of rulers, they give us a picture of the serfs' conditions. And as the explanations of the sixty-four hexagrams in *The Book of Change* have a folk origin, they too supply us with much general information about life in those days. Thus there are references to fishing and hunting, husbandry and agriculture, war, sacrifice and marriage, food and drink, housing and clothing. If we disregard the many mystical commentaries and false interpretations of these books written in the past, they remain important prose works of the early Zhou dynasty.

2. Warring States Period

The works of the Warring States Period are entirely unlike the earlier Zhou literature.

After the Spring and Autumn Period, there was a change in the system of landownership and gradually a new landlord class appeared. In the course of the struggle between these new landowners and the old feudal chiefs, the literati emerged as a prominent group and began to dominate all cultural activities. More important still, after the Zhou people advanced eastwards from the Wei River to the Yellow River Valley, even the Yangtse Valley changed. And when the kingdom of Chu with its distinctive traditions came within the economic orbit of the Zhou empire, this greatly hastened the spread of culture.

The most outstanding literature of this period is *Chu Ci*, the poetry of the kingdom of Chu.

These poems were written in the dialect of Chu and set to Chu music. The earliest are the *Nine Odes* — actually

Qu Yuan, portrait by Chen Hongshou
(1599-1652)

eleven in number — used in sacrifices in the kingdom of Chu at the end of the Spring and Autumn Period and the beginning of the Warring States Period. The deities and spirits to whom sacrifices were made were for the most part gods and goddesses related to agriculture: the sun god, the cloud god, or mountain and water goddesses. As the ancients believed that gods were like men and could fall in love with mortals, the *Nine Odes* also speak of love. Through the love of shamans for gods and goddesses, they expressed men's longing for richer gifts from nature: if the gods were pleased they would surely send better harvests, if angry they would destroy the crops. The "Ode to the Fallen" was used in sacrifices to the warriors who had fallen in battle, and shows the people's profound love for their country. It is possible that the great poet Qu Yuan may have rewritten these odes, but they are generally considered as the work, in the main, of anonymous poets.

Soon after the *Nine Odes* were composed lived the brilliant poet Qu Yuan, a noble of the kingdom of Chu. The date of his birth is uncertain, but it was probably between 343 and 339 B.C. At about the age of twenty he began to take part in affairs of state. At home he advocated the promotion of able ministers, and in foreign policy an alliance with the state of Qi against the growing power of Qin. Such a policy was in the best interests of his kingdom, but as it was detrimental to certain nobles of Chu and to the state of Qin, wicked men, in league with the envoys sent by Qin slandered Qu Yuan and succeeded in having him banished. First he was exiled to north of the Han River, then — when he was nearing fifty — to south of the Yangtse. When he saw that his country was approaching ruin yet he could do nothing to save it, he felt great despair and drowned himself in the Miluo River near Lake Dongting. Tradition has it that he died on the fifth day of the fifth month, and he is commemorated on the Dragon-Boat Festival which falls on that day, but the year of his death is unknown. It was probably about 280 B.C., for in 278 B.C. the Qin army stormed the capital of Chu, and it is certain that Qu Yuan would not have lived on after this disgrace.

His masterpiece is the *Li Sao*, a poem of more than three hundred and seventy lines, which sets forth his aspirations and emotions. It is beautifully constructed, with considerable variety in the sentence structure and magnificent imagery. The theme of the poem is clear. Qu Yuan expresses his sincere love for his country and concern for his countrymen, ruthlessly exposing the king's folly and the treachery of evil ministers. He uses fragrant herbs to symbolize his own aspiring spirit.

> *With lavished innate qualities indued,*
> *By art and skill my talents I renewed;*

> *Angelic herbs and sweet selineas too,*
> *And orchids late that by the water grew,*
> *I wove for ornament, till fleeting time*
> *Like water flowing stole away my prime.**

Though he met with many setbacks and occasionally was on the verge of despair, his fervent patriotism made him fight on resolutely:

> *In exile rather would I meet my end*
> *Than to the baseness of their ways descend.*
> *Remote the eagle spurns the common range,*
> *Nor deigns since time began its way to change;*
> *A circle fits not with a square design:*
> *Their different ways could not be merged with mine.*
> *Yet still my heart I checked and curbed my pride,*
> *Their blame endured and their reproach beside.*
> *To die for righteousness alone I sought,*
> *For this was what the ancient sages taught.*

He has left us an incomparably moving picture of a patriot of ancient times.

Qu Yuan also wrote the *Nine Elegies* and the *Riddles*, another long poem in which he poses more than a hundred questions. Some of these are concerned with natural phenomena such as the creation of heaven and earth, or the rising and setting of the sun and moon; some deal with ancient myths and legends; some relate to historical figures. Qu Yuan's approach is sceptical and realistic for a man of his day, and this poem has preserved many ancient myths and legends for us. The *Nine Elegies* are short lyrics about the poet's own experiences and difficulties. His feelings are strong and his language passionate. The same love for his

---

* This and the following translations of Qu Yuan's poems are quoted from *Li Sao and Other Peoms of Chu Yuan* (Foreign Languages Press, 1955), translated by Yang Hsien-yi and Gladys Yang.

country and anguish over its fate expressed in the *Li Sao* can be found in these poems.

> *Now, the phoenix dispossessed,*
> *In the shrine crows make their nest.*
> *Withered is the jasmine rare,*
> *Fair is foul, and foul is fair,*
> *Light is darkness, darkness day,*
> *Sad at heart I haste away.*
>
> ("Crossing the River")

When banished south of the Yangtse he lamented:

> *High Heav'n proves fickle once again,*
> *And showers calamities like rain.*
> *Homes are destroyed and loved ones die,*
> *As east in early spring we fly.*
>
> ("Leaving the Capital")

Though he was hounded to his death, his immortal poems will always live on to inspire fresh generations of patriots.

Qu Yuan was succeeded by the poets Tang Le, Jing Chai and Song Yu; but only Song Yu's work remains today. Song Yu is said to have been Qu Yuan's student and to have served in the court of Chu. Judging by his *Nine Arguments*, he started life as a poverty-stricken scholar, who was slandered after he became an official so that he lost his position. The *Nine Arguments* is a long poem written after he fell from favour, and in it he made it clear that he would not compromise with evil. A long poem, *Requiem*, attributed to either Song Yu or Qu Yuan, was written to call back the spirit of the king after his death. It contrasts the sufferings of the people in neighbouring states with the prosperity of his own.

> *Among the damsels sit the guests all down;*
> *Abandons each his belt and tasseled crown;*
> *In wanton wise the damsels make display;*

The girl disguised as warrior wins the day.
Then draughts they play, and chess with ivory wrought,
Divided all in pairs the games are fought;
The die is cast, they call the gods for aid;
They revel long until the day doth fade.
Some strike the urn and knock the wood frame o'er,
Some play the slanting lyre and sing once more;
Still wine they urge, forgetting night or day;
Within the bright lamp burns the orchid grey.
With skill and optness, as with fragrance sweet,
They chant the songs for such occasion meet;
They drink to crown their joy and praise the past.
Return, O soul, homeward return at last!

In addition, Song Yu is believed by certain scholars to have written some narrative poetry; but here again the authenticity is dubious. The *Nine Arguments* shows that Song Yu followed the tradition of Qu Yuan, and these two men are the greatest poets of the later Zhou period.

During this time China also had many prose writers who have left us two main categories of work: historical records and philosophical writing.

The four chief historical works are *The Spring and Autumn Annals*, *Zuo Zhuan*, *Guo Yu* and *Guo Ce*. *The Spring and Autumn Annals* is a brief chronological record made by official historians of the state of Lu, dealing with the chief events of the early Eastern Zhou period. Confucius used this book to teach his pupils but was probably not its author. Since these records are very brief, their literary value is slight.

The *Zuo Zhuan* and the *Guo Yu*, which record the history of the same period, are more detailed. As literature, the *Zuo Zhuan* surpasses the others. It gives vivid and truthful accounts of the extravagance and cruelty of certain tyrants, convincing sketches of heroes and famous statesmen, and sympathetic descriptions of the life of the common man. The accounts of battle scenes are famous for the brilliant economy of language with which the author presents complex situations. For instance, when the states of Qin and Jin were about to join battle at Yao, the Qin army decided to make a surprise attack on the state of Zheng. Passing the north gate of Eastern Zhou, they behaved so insolently that even children prophesied their defeat; and before they reached Zheng their purpose was discovered:

At Hua they were met by a merchant of Zheng named Xuan Gao, who was travelling on business to the city of Zhou. He presented them with four hides and twelve oxen. "Our prince has heard that your forces mean to pass our humble city and respectfully offers these to your men," said the merchant. "Our humble state is not rich, but for your entertainment we shall prepare one day's food if you stay, or provide one night's sentry service if you are moving on." And he sent a swift messenger to the city of Zheng.

Since Zheng was now prepared, the Qin army turned back to be defeated by the forces of Jin, and three of their generals were captured. This narrative not only gives a detailed account of the campaign, but a picture of the merchant's ready wit and patriotism. The *Guo Yu* is less graphic. Both these works, traditionally attributed to Zuoqiu Ming, are in fact from the hand of unknown writers of the Warring States Period.

The *Guo Ce* is a later work. It records events during the Warring States Period, the various alliances, the struggles between the old and new landowners, the activities of the literati, the economic prosperity of the states and the sufferings of the labouring people. The *Guo Ce* includes a number of fables, like the one related by Su Dai to King Hui of Zhao, who was about to attack the state of Yan, not realizing that the king of Qin hoped to take advantage of their quarrel:

A mussel was opening its shell to bask in the sun when a snipe pecked at it. The mussel clamped down on the bird's beak, and held it fast. "If it doesn't rain tomorrow," said the snipe, "there will be a dead mussel lying here." "If you can't prize loose today or tomorrow," retorted the mussel, "there will be a dead snipe here too." As neither of them would give way, a passing fisherman caught them both.

Even today in China allusion is often made to this fight between the mussel and the snipe. "Drawing a Snake with Legs" and "The Fox Who Profited by the Tiger's Might" are among the other colourful and compact fables with a pointed moral taken from the *Guo Ce*.

Another important branch of prose was that written by philosophers of the period to propagate their ideas. These thinkers represented different class interests. The group headed by Confucius was called the Ru school. Confucius came from the nobility which was declining, and in the realm of ideas tried to retain many features of the old system, though he had to make certain concessions in view of the changing circumstances and the rise of new land-owners. Some of his proposals, therefore, hastened the destruction of the old. In the feudal society which lasted for more than two thousand years in China, the Confucian philosophy formed the ideological basis of the ruling class, justifying its control of the people. Confucius had many disciples, and their propagation of knowledge played a positive role in the formation and development of Chinese culture. His chief successors were Mencius and Xun Zi. The sayings of Confucius were recorded by his disciples in the *Analects*. Two other books have preserved the teachings of Mencius and Xun Zi. The *Analects* consists of short sayings only, and the style is simple and straightforward, but there are some lively discussions between Confucius and his disciples. Here is a typical passage from the beginning of the second book:

The Master said: He who rules by moral force is like the pole-star, which remains in its place while all the lesser stars do homage to it.

The Master said: If out of the three hundred *Songs* I had to take one phrase to cover all my teaching, I would say, "Let there be no evil in your thoughts."

The Master said: Govern the people by regulations, keep order among them by chastisements, and they will flee from you, and lose all self-respect. Govern them by moral force, keep order among them by ritual and they will keep their self-respect and come to you of their own accord.

The Master said: At fifteen I set my heart upon learning. At thirty, I had planted my feet firm upon the ground. At forty, I no longer suffered from perplexities. At fifty, I knew what were the biddings of Heaven. At sixty, I heard them with docile ear. At seventy, I could follow the dictates of my own heart; for what I desired no longer overstepped the boundaries of right.*

The *Book of Mencius* is written in more varied and eloquent prose, and some of the arguments there are carefully reasoned. The story of the man of Qi and his two wives is well known. This man boasted that every day he feasted with rich men or nobles, but the women did not believe him.

The wife said to the concubine: "Each time our good man goes out he comes back replete with wine and meat, and when we ask where he has feasted he says with rich men and nobles. But not a single gentleman of quality has been here. I mean to find out where he goes." The next morning, accordingly, she followed her husband when he left the house; but not a soul in the city spoke to him. At last he approached some mourners who were sacrificing at a grave in the east suburb, to beg for what remained of their offerings. Not satisfied with this, he accosted some mourners until he had filled his belly. The wife went home and told the concubine: "We looked to our husband

---

* From *The Analects of Confucius* translated by Arthur Waley.

to provide for us all our life, but this is the sort of fellow he is!" Then they abused him roundly and wept in the courtyard till the husband, all unaware of this, swaggered home and started boasting to them again.

This is a satire on those who stoop to base deeds in order to secure wealth and comfort, and later writers used this story in plays or ballads to attack different social abuses. Though Mencius supported the feudal system, his contention that "the people come first" had a positive significance.

Xun Zi advocated the use of ceremony and punishment, and attacked fatalism and superstition. His philosophy, further developed by his disciples, provided the theoretical basis of the political centralism of the Qin and Han dynasties. His prose is succinct and logical compared with that of Mencius, as can be seen from this passage:

The nature of man is evil — his goodness is only acquired by training. The original nature of man today is to seek for gain. If this desire is followed, strife and rapacity result and courtesy dies. Man originally is envious and naturally hates others. If these tendencies are followed, injury and destruction result, loyalty and faithfulness are destroyed. Man originally possessed the desires of the ear and the eye; he likes praise and is lustful. If these are followed, impurity and disorder result, and the rules of proper conduct, justice and refined culture are done away with. Therefore to give rein to man's original nature, to follow man's feelings, inevitably results in strife and rapacity, together with violations of good customs and confusion in the proper way of doing things: there is reversion to a state of violence. Hence the civilizing influence of teachers and laws, the guidance of the rites and justice, is absolutely necessary. Thereupon courtesy appears, cultured behaviour is observed, and good government is the consequence. By this line of argument it is evident that the nature of man is evil and his goodness is acquired.*

There were many schools of thought in addition to the Confucian, chief of them the Mohist, Daoist and Legalist. Their writings include *Mo Zi* by Mo Di and his disciples, the *Dao De Jing* by Li Er, *Zhuang Zi* by Zhuang Zhou and his disciples, *Han Fei Zi* by Han Fei and others. The Mohists, who opposed the Confucians, were closer to the common people, and the prose of *Mo Zi* is simple and unadorned.

Li Er and Zhuang Zhou were Daoists, who attacked the feudal system but looked back to a primitive agrarian collectivism. Their teachings contain the roots of Chinese scientific thought and concepts of democracy. Thus Li Er had some understanding of the contradictions in the objective world. The *Dao De Jing* is written in succinct and beautiful language, with graphic images to illustrate profound ideas. Here, for instance, is a vivid description of the dialectics of Nature:

> *Among the creatures of the world some go in front,*
> *   some follow;*
> *Some blow hot when others would be blowing cold;*
> *Some are feeling vigorous just when others are worn out,*
> *Some are loading just when others are delivering,*
> *Therefore the sage discards the "absolute," the "all-*
> *   inclusive," the "extreme."***

Zhuang Zhou's prose is swift and lively, sometimes sublime. Instead of direct statements of fact, he often uses anecdotes. Daring imagination and acute observation make all his work superbly alive. The tale of the cook who cut up bullocks is a good example of his style.

Lord Wen Hui's cook was cutting up a bullock. Each blow of his hands, each heave of his shoulders, each tread of his feet, each thrust of his knees, each whish of sliced

---

* From Chapter XXIII of *The Works of Hsun Tzu* translated by H.H. Dubs.

**From *The Way and Its Power*, translated by Arthur Waley.

flesh, each swish of the cleaver was in perfect harmony. . . . "Admirable!" cried Lord Wen Hui. "Yours is skill indeed!" The cook laid down his cleaver and replied: "Your servant loves the Way, which is better than skill. When I first began to cut up bullocks, I saw simply the whole carcase; but after three years' practice, I saw no more whole animals. Now I work with my brain, not my eyes. . . . At a touch of my cleaver the flesh comes away from the bone like earth crumbling to the ground. Then standing with cleaver in hand I gaze round in triumph before wiping my cleaver and putting it away." "Bravo!" cried Lord Wen Hui. "From the words of this cook I have learned how to preserve life."

This delightful anecdote illustrates the need to grasp the objective laws of Nature. Because the cook understood the bullocks's anatomy, after nineteen years of use his cleaver was as good as new. The descriptions in *Zhuang Zi* are always graphic and convincing.

Han Fei, the chief exponent of the Legalists, was a disciple of Xun Zi, who opposed the old nobility and supported the new landowners. His style is precise and he shows penetrating powers of analysis. His writings embody many persuasive fables and parables like "Buying the Casket Without the Pearl," "The Shield and the Spear," and "Waiting for the Hare."

This period also saw the beginning of stories and drama.

The origin of fiction is closely linked with myths and legends which, at first handed down by word of mouth, were gradually recorded as written literature. Some of these have been preserved in *The Book of Songs* and the *Chu Ci*, and many more in *The Book of Mountains and Seas*. Although the old literati attributed this work to the legendary Yu or Yi, it was actually written during the Warring States Period, some sections being added during the Qin and Han dynasties. While intended as a geographical record, it contains less fact than fiction, and its accounts of different mountains and

Illustration from an old edition of The Book of Mountains and Seas *published about 1615*

streams embody beautiful legends, some with a deep meaning like the story of the bird called *jingwei*.

> Two hundred *li* to the north stands Fajiu Mountain, its sides covered with *zhe* trees. There is a bird there like a crow with white beak and red feet, called *jingwei* from the sound it makes when it cries. This bird was Nü Wa, the young daughter of Yan Di, who was drowned while swimming in the Eastern Ocean and transformed into a bird. All day it carries wood and stones from the Western Hill to fill up the sea. The Zhang River rises here, flowing eastwards to the Yellow River.

This myth also reflects our forbears' determination to conquer nature, and their courage in the face of obstacles.

Another work of this period is *The Travels of King Mu* by an unknown writer. A mixture of history and fancy, this is based on the legend that King Mu of the Zhou dynasty travelled all over the world. The different places he visited are listed, and the king is described as a monarch who would listen to advice and have his subjects' welfare at heart. The real King Mu was probably not such a good ruler, but by writing in this way the author showed his longing to better the lot of the people.

The fables imbedded in so many of these historical and philosophical writings, some of which have been quoted, also gave great impetus to the rise of fiction.

Drama arose from ritual dances miming certain stories. These dances, often closely connected with production and fertility, formed the main part of many sacrificial ceremonies. As these ancient rites frequently took the form of primitive dramas, it is to them that we must look for the origin of Chinese drama. *The Book of Songs* and the *Chu Ci* shed some light on this question. At first the performers were witches or shamans whose purpose it was to please the gods, and they were succeeded by clowns who performed dramatic dances to entertain men. Clowns appeared very early in China, but did not become generally popular till the Warring States Period. They were proficient dancers, musicians, jesters and acrobats, whose influence on later drama was considerable.

From this brief survey of the literature of the Zhou dynasty, it can be seen that poetry was pre-eminent—this age produced immortal poems and poets. Prose developed too, mainly in the form of philosophical or historical writing of a markedly didactic and humanistic character, while fiction and drama were only just beginning. But the fine tradition of classical Chinese literature had already emerged, and conditions were favourable for its development.

The Travels of King Mu

III. Literature of the Qin, Han, Wei and Jin Dynasties, and the Southern and Northern Dynasties

1. Qin and Han Dynasties

After the Spring and Autumn Period the old economy was gradually superseded by the new landlord economy, and in the third century B.C. Qin Shi Huang Di, First Emperor of Qin, united all China and set up the first autocratic feudal empire in Chinese history. The next eight hundred years, from this time till the end of the sixth century, may be considered as the third stage in the development of classical Chinese literature.

The unification of China marked a great historical advance. During this period the borders of the empire were extended and the population increased. Agriculture improved, and handicrafts and commerce developed. Many scientific discoveries were made, including the invention of paper and the compass. The landowners, who held the political power generation after generation, had a virtual monopoly of culture; and the *élite* of this class lived in considerable luxury. But the peasants, burdened by heavy taxation and military conscription, led such a hard life that these eight hundred years saw a succession of peasant revolts.

The Qin dynasty lasted a mere fifteen years, and its only well-known writer was Li Si, but his work is not of the first order. The Han dynasty produced the famous historian Sima Qian, a master of classical Chinese prose.

司馬遷像

Sima Qian

Sima Qian was a native of Longmen in present-day Shaanxi, who was born in about 140 B.C. and died at the beginning of the first century B.C. His father was the court astrologer and historian, and Sima Qian succeeded him to this post. To gather historical material, he travelled all over China and visited the descendants or friends of famous men. Later he was punished for defending a general in disgrace, but in order to complete his great work he endured this indignity patiently. That immortal classic, the *Records of the Historian*, is the result of his painstaking work and brilliant powers of observation and analysis.

Records of the Historian is the first general Chinese history, and in it Sima Qian has given us a graphic and systematic account of many historical occurrences and social changes.

His inspired pen brings complex historical events to life, and has presented us with a gallery of unsurpassed portraits of the highest and the lowest in the land. Thus the story of how Lin Xiangru saved the state of Zhao is known throughout China today thanks to Sima Qian. Lin Xiangru was a minor official during the Warring States Period, whose king possessed a precious jade emblem which the king of Qin coveted. The king of Qin offered fifteen cities for this jade; but though this was clearly a trick, Qin was so powerful that the king of Zhao did not known how to refuse. Then Lin Xiangru volunteered to go to Qin to negotiate, promising to bring back either fifteen cities or the jade. This is how Sima Qian describes his behaviour in the Qin court:

> Seeing that the king did not mean to give Zhao the cities, Xiangru stepped forward and said: "There is a flaw in this jade. Let me show it to Your Majesty." When the king handed him the jade, he took his stand with his back against a pillar. His hair bristled with rage and he cried: ". . . As Your Majesty has no intention of giving these cities to Zhao, I have taken back the jade. Try to get it from me by force, and I shall break both my head and the jade against this prillar!" With a glance at the pillar he held up the jade, and made ready to smash it.

The characterization here is magnificent. Lin Xiangru's courage, ingenuity and patriotism are strongly presented with great economy of language. And his outstanding ability as an envoy explains how this low-ranking functionary came to be appointed chief minister of Zhao. But Lian Po, a famous general of Zhao, had no respect for him and tried to humiliate him. When Lin Xiangru knew of this, he did his best to keep out of Lian Po's way. And when his followers protested, he explained:

> Though the king of Qin is mighty, I bellowed at him in his court and made free with his ministers. Weak though I am, why should I fear General Lian? But the

two of us are the sole reason why powerful Qin dare not invade Zhao. If two tigers fight, one must perish. I take this stand because I put our country first and private grudges second.

These magnanimous words moved the general, who went to Lin Xiangru to apologize, and after that the two men became firm friends. Sima Qian has not only given a vivid and convincing picture of two patriots, but by the masterly realism of his descriptions has brought these old heroes to life. Because he chooses the events of the greatest consequence in his recording of history, all his characters have a broad significance. Moreover, his strong views and clear sense of right and wrong give great depth of feeling to his writing and make the scenes he portrays unforgettable. This is why we prize the *Records* as a literary masterpiece as well as a great history.

A successor to Sima Qian was Ban Gu, who wrote the *Han Dynasty History*. Ban Gu was native of Anling in present-day Shaanxi, who lived from A.D. 32 to 92. His father, Ban Biao, and his younger sister, Ban Zhao, helped him to collect the materials for this history, but he did most of the actual writing himself. He had a more conservative outlook than Sima Qian; but his prose, while not so brilliant, is concise and fluent. He too has left us authentic and affecting character sketches of historical figures. For example, there is Su Wu who would not let Wei Lü prevail on him to surrender to the Huns.

When Su Wu made no answer, Wei Lü said: "If you take my advice and surrender, we shall become sworn brothers. If you turn a deaf ear, you shall never see me again." Then Su Wu swore at him: "I never want to set eyes on you again — a subject who has forgotten his sovereign's kindness and betrayed him by going over to the barbarians. . . ." When Wei Lü saw that he could not be persuaded, he reported this to the khan, who became more eager than ever to master Su. Thereupon they imprisoned him in a great dungeon, without food or drink. It snowed, and by swallowing snow and chewing felt as he lay there, Su Wu did not die for some days, to all the Huns' amazement.

A gifted contemporary of Ban Gu was the outstanding thinker Wang Chong, a native of Shangyu in present-day Zhejiang. He was born in A.D. 27 and died at the end of the first century. As his family was relatively poor, it was not easy for him to study, but he served as a minor official and taught in a school. His sceptical, rationalist philosophy is largely embodied in *Discourses Weighed in the Balance* which he wrote to combat current superstitions and the schools of thought which served the interests of the land-

Wang Chong, wood-block print dated 1856

owning class. He had the courage to attack Confucius and Mencius, the sages of feudal society, and to oppose corrupt and evil officials. There are elements of materialism in his thinking, and his approach to literature is an enlightened one, as we see from this passage in his writing:

Jade within a rock or a pearl hidden in the belly of a fish cannot be seen; but when the jade glitters from the heart of the rock or the pearl gleams through the belly of the fish, their radiance cannot be hidden. So my thoughts, when not recorded but kept in my heart, are like hidden jade and pearls. Appearing, they are like jade and pearls revealing their brightness . . . . Literature should be hard to write but easy to grasp: there is no merit in facile writing which is obscure. Arguments should settle problems and be persuasive: they serve no purpose if involved and unintelligible.

Wang Chong put this theory into practice. Because his language is clear and fluent and his syntax concise, his arguments are persuasive. At a time when a euphuistic style of writing was coming into favour, his prose had a distinctive simplicity.

Many writers in the Han dynasty wrote *fu*, a descriptive poetic prose interspersed with verse. This literary form arose among the people and was then taken up by scholars, who cultivated a euphuistic style. There was much competent writing of this sort, but little of it is genuine literature. The folk-songs known as *yue fu*, most of which have five words to a line, are much more outstanding than the *fu* of this period.

Yue fu originally meant the office in charge of music during the Han dynasty. Since the folk-songs collected by this office had a great influence on writers, by degrees all such songs came to be known as *yue fu*, and these folk-songs of the Han and the Southern and Northern Dynasties are an important part of China's cultural heritage.

Many of the Han folk-songs describe the life of humble folk and their problems. "East Gate" tells the story of a poor couple who can not make a living and decide to become brigands. "The Sick Wife" describes how a man whose wife has died of illness tries to care for his motherless children. "Song of the Orphan" recounts the sufferings of a boy at the hands of his elder brother and sister-in-law:

> *Sent to draw water at dawn,*
> *I don't get home till dusk;*
> *Hands chapped and bleeding,*
> *Feet bare,*
> *I walk the frosty earth,*
> *Plucking out thorns by the thousand—*
> *But still the pain throbs on.*
> *In bitterness*
> *My tears fall*
> *Pearl after pearl.*
> *In winter I have no coat,*
> *In summer no shirt . . . .*

Other songs tell of the horrors of war. Thus "Fighting South of the Castle" begins:

> *They fought south of the Castle;*
> *They died north of the Wall.*
> *They died in the moors and were not buried.*
> *Their flesh was the food of crows.**

"I Fought for My Lord at Fifteen" is the song of a man who has served as a soldier for sixty-five years, who finds all his relatives dead when he goes home. These poignant, haunting lyrics are among the finest work of the Han dynasty. They appeal to men's finest sympathies, and their natural yet beautiful form was an inspiration to countless later writers.

---

* From *170 Chinese Poems*, translated by Arthur Waley.

This period saw further development in fiction and drama. Some of the fiction attributed to Han dynasty authors is actually of a later date. There are, however, some genuine Han works of fiction which have not traditionally been classified as such. Thus *Anecdotes on the Book of Songs* by Han Ying, and *The Garden of Anecdotes* and *New Discourses* by Liu Xiang contain many short tales which point a moral and are good stories into the bargain. Similarly *The Lost History of Yue* by Yuan Kang and Wu Ping and *Annals of Wu and Yue* by Zhao Ye may be considered as historical romances. They show a further development from *The Travels of King Mu*.

The advance of the drama was not so marked. During the Han dynasty there were acrobatic and puppet shows performed by jesters. The acrobatic shows had a popular origin and were combined with stories, songs and dances. The puppet shows are believed to have started as rites to exorcize demons, but they took shape as plays and became a form of popular entertainment, continuing to be a favourite amusement after the Han dynasty.

2. Wei, Jin, and the Southern and Northern Dynasties

During the Wei and Jin dynasties, there were further changes in the form and content of Chinese literature. A class of professional writers came into being, more anthologies of poetry and essays were edited, and an increasing volume of literary criticism appeared.

At the same time a decadent tendency was evident. Many writers paid more attention to the choice of words and images and the use of classical allusions and parallelisms than to the content of their work.

Since most of the *yue fu* of the Han dynasty had five words to the line, this form now came into general use; and the realism of these folk-songs influenced and inspired later poets. The most famous poets of this period are Cao Zhi of the Three Kingdoms, Tao Yuanming of the Jin dynasty, and

Bao Zhao of the Southern and Northern Dynasties.

Cao Zhi (192-232) was the precocious son of the famous general and statesman Cao Cao. His brother, Cao Pi, was jealous of him, and while Cao Pi was emperor he treated Cao Zhi badly. Finding it impossible to realize his political ambitions, the poet expressed his frustration in literature, notably in verse.

Cao Zhi was a contemporary of the "Seven Poets of the Jian An Period" headed by Wang Can. These men, growing up in the unsettled times at the end of the Han dynasty, captured the spirit of the *yue fu* and succeeded in writing poems which give a true picture of their day. Of these poets Cao Zhi was the best, yet even his early poems—written while he was still living the life of a young nobleman—lack profundity. In his later years, after he had suffered much, he wrote with deeper feeling. In "To Biao, Prince of Baima," he exposes the factions and strife that split the ruling class:

> *Owls hoot before your carriage;*
> *Wolves and jackals prowl the road;*
> *Flies change spotlessness into filth,*
> *And even the hearts of dear ones*
> *Are poisoned by slander.*

His own afflictions made him aware of the deeper sufferings of the common people. Thus elsewhere we find him writing:

> *Pity the coastal dwellers*
> *In their wild, reedy country;*
> *Their children and their wives seem scarcely human,*
> *Lurking in mountain retreats.*

In other poems he expressed his political aspirations and his love for his motherland.

Tao Yuanming, or Tao Qian, was a native of Chaisang in present-day Jiangxi. He was born between 365 and 372, and died in 427. He came of an impoverished landowning family, was a man of integrity and served in a minor official

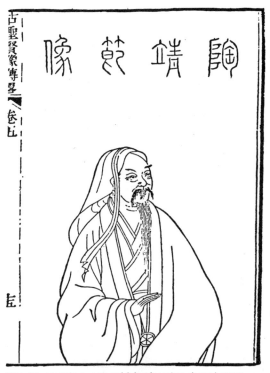

Tao Yuanming, wood-block print dated 1830

capacity until 405, when he retired to live on his farm. This brought him close to the peasants, for he tilled the soil himself and often suffered cold and hunger. These experiences made him view life differently from other writers of his class. His profound understanding coupled with his brilliant literary gifts made him the greatest poet of the Jin dynasty and one of the greatest writers in all Chinese history.

Most of the poets popular during the Jin dynasty, such as Lu Ji and Pan Yue, emphasized form at the expense of content. Indeed, this was the way to win fame at that time. Xie Lingyun and Yan Yanzhi, who lived a little later than Tao Yuanming, wrote brilliant poems— Xie Lingyun's nature poems are much celebrated—yet sometimes their verses are marred by excessive ornateness. In this age when florid, artificial language was the fashion, Tao Yuanming was the only poet to use simple, everyday speech to write of daily life. An example of this is "Harvesting Early Rice in the West Field in the Ninth Month of the Year Geng Xu (Keng hsu)":

After spring my round of labour begins anew
And I can look ahead to my yearly harvest.
Out with the dawn, exerting all my strength,
Home at sunset bearing my plough on my shoulder . . . .
How can it not be hard, this farmer's life?
And the hardship is such that no one can avoid.
So tired is my whole body when I come home,
That I cannot even think of other troubles. . . . *

Again in his "Miscellaneous Poems" he writes:

. . . I never wished to receive on official's pay,
The fields and mulberry trees are my profession.
I work myself, taking no rest:
Sometimes in hunger and cold I have eaten chaff.

By such descriptions Tao Yuanming gives us a truthful picture of the hard conditions of the peasants at the time, who often went cold and hungry to satisfy the greed of the landowners. He also wrote about poverty-stricken scholars, sketching the life of other poor men like himself. Living in the country, he had friends among the labouring people. Thus he wrote in "Moving Home":

When work in the fields is done, each one goes home;
And then at leisure I think again of friends.
I think of friends—and fling my cloak on my shoulder;
For never we tire of talk and laughter together.

Clearly he was not one of the feudal scholars who viewed

---

* Translated by Andrew Boyd.

things from the standpoint of the landlords and distorted the truth about the peasants.

His poems express different moods and deal with a great variety of topics. Even-tempered and open-minded, he often gave himself up to drinking as if he had no worldly cares or serious interests in life. He has been called a hermit poet because his poems to the snow or the chrysanthemum express his own emotions or his joy at feeling at one with the universe. In fact, however, he followed political events closely and was deeply concerned over the fate of the country. The verses he wrote on the ancient gallant, Jing Ke or the mythical bird that tried to fill up the ocean show that he was by no means the escapist that he has been made out. Indeed, as Lu Xun points out, Tao Yuanming was a great poet.

Bao Zhao was a native of Donghai in present-day Jiangsu. He was born in about 410 and killed by rebel troops in 466. He came from an impoverished family, and though while little more than a boy he gave evidence of considerable literary talent, he was not highly regarded by the more influential literati. Even after he won fame, the envy of his contemporaries made it difficult for him to develop his gifts; thus his poems often voice indignation:

> At table I cannot eat:
> I strike the pillar with my sword and sigh—
> How long is man's span of life?
> How can I curb my step and fold my wings?
> Far better to give up an official career,
> Go home and live at ease . . . .
> The sages of old were destitute and obscure,
> Much more so candid and honest men today!

Sometimes he made direct attacks upon the iniquities of the government:

> I bind faggots in the shady bamboo glade,
> Reap millet in the chilly valley;

The north wind cuts right through me,
And bird-cries startle me.
Before the New Year taxes must be paid,
And at other times different levies:
The land tax must be sent to Hanku Pass,
With fodder for the beasts in the royal parks.
. . . Officers scourge us with rods,
And bailiffs shout insults at us.

Unlike most poets of his time, who cultivated a precious style and admired a decadent way of life, Bao Zhao learned from folk-songs and was a spokesman of the people, although certain of his poems contain parallelisms and are tainted by euphuism.

After this, strict patterns were gradually introduced for classical poetry, rules were made to govern the use of the four tones, and parallelisms were encouraged. Xie Tiao and Yu Xin did much to popularize this style, but their own work is not of the first order.

During the Wei and Jin dynasties more fiction was written, of a higher standard than heretofore. It fell into two main categories: stories about the supernatural, and anecdotes about famous men. *Records of Spirits* by Gan Bao is an example of the former, and *New Anecdotes* by Liu Yiqing of the latter.

Gan Bao was a native of Xincai in present-day Henan, who lived approximately from 285 to 360. Some of his tales are based on historical records, others have a folk origin. A number of them reflect man's struggle against Nature or resistance to oppression. His story of the sword-maker's son is well known.

. . . "You are young," the stranger said. "Why do you weep so bitterly?" "I am the son of Ganjiang and Moye," replied the lad. "The king of Chu killed my father. I want revenge." "I hear the king has offered a thousand gold pieces for your head," said the stranger. "Give me your

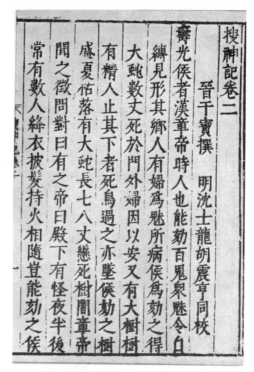

An old edition of Records of Spirits *published about 1603*

head and your sword, and I will avenge you." "Very well," agreed the boy. Then he killed himself and, standing erect, presented his head and his sword with both hands to the stranger. Then the lad fell dead to the ground.

This tale goes on to describe how the wicked king was killed and the sword-maker avenged.

Liu Yiqing (403-444) was a native of Pengcheng in present-day Jiangsu. His *New Anecdotes* deal with the conversation and behaviour of historical figures. By means of graphic and truthful descriptions he conjures up these men for us with all their personal idiosyncrasies, and sheds light on the customs of the time and the luxurious mode of life of the rulers.

Some of the best books dealing with the supernatural are *The Garden of Marvels* by Liu Jingshu and *Supplement to the Tales of Qi* by Wu Jun. *Tales* by Yin Yun and *Merry Stories* by Hou Bai are in a similar vein to the *New Anecdotes*.

Most of the prose writers of this period, like the poets, tended to sacrifice content to formal beauty. This was not the case, however, with the two famous writers Fan Zhen of the Southern Dynasties and Li Daoyuan of the Northern Dynasties. Fan Zhen was a native of Wuyin in present-day Henan, who was born in about 450 and died early in the sixth century. He inherited and carried forward the materialist tradition of Wang Chong, and his celebrated essay *On the Destructibility of the Soul* caused a sensation. He argued that human life is inseparable from man's physical existence, and that therefore after death all mental activities must cease. "The soul is to the body what sharpness is to a knife," he said. "I have never heard that after the knife is destroyed the sharpness can persist." He lashed out also at the superstition and selfishness rife among ruling circles, and his eloquence, which spread confusion among officials, made common folk rejoice. Li Daoyuan was a native of Zhuolu in present-day Hepei. The date of his birth is uncertain, but he died in 527. In his masterpiece, *The Commentary to the Canon of Rivers*, he conjures up an enthralling picture of famous mountains and streams and China's magnificent scenery. As he was a northerner, his descriptions of the Yellow River Valley are more detailed than those of the south — a sign that he based his writing on personal observation and verified reports.

During the Southern and Northern Dynasties the best of a number of good works of literary criticism was Liu Xie's *Carving a Dragon at the Core of Literature*. Liu Xie was a native of Chu in present-day Shandong, who lived from about 465 to 520. Though his ancestors had served as officials he was not rich, and his masterpiece was not highly regarded by his contemporaries. In this outstanding work he makes a comprehensive and systematic study of the literary forms, styles, authors and works of various dynasties. He points out that different ages produce different types of writing, while the divergence of individual personality results in different styles. Again and again he condemns the undue emphasis currently laid on such embellishments as parallelisms, allusions or rhythm. Thus he writes: "Too many flowers spoil the bough, too much fat is bad for the bone. Writings of this type are vulgar, and neither make good models nor serve any moral purpose." Again: "When the ideas are lean but the language is padded out, a work seems an incongruous farrago, and no main skeleton or outline is visible. ... These men study and emulate magnificent bombast to the exclusion of all else beside, and are completely carried away by this." He expresses these sound views forcefully and graphically, with great economy of language.

Zhong Rong's *Critique of Poetry* and certain sections of Yan Zhitui's *Yan Family Admonitions* were also valuable contributions to literary criticism.

Finally we come to the folk-songs and dances or early dramas of this period.

During the Southern and Northern Dynasties most songs of the south were love songs, while those of the north dealt mainly with the horrors of war. Here is a southern lyric about silkworms:

> *Spring silkworms never weary,*
> *But spin their longing night and day;*
> *What matter if they perish*
> *Since love can never pass away?*

And here is a northern song:

> *Ah, man is born to sorrow,*
> *And leaves his home to die;*
> *His corpse is lost upon the hill,*
> *His bones unburied lie!*

The southern songs are tender and passionate compared with the simpler northern lyrics.

Two long folk-songs deserve special mention. One is *The Bride of Jiao Zhongqing*, otherwise known as *South-east the Peacock Flies*, which describes the tragic love story of a couple who lived at the end of the Han dynasty. Lanzhi was a beautiful and intelligent girl who discharged her household duties admirably, yet her mother-in-law disliked her and forced her son to divorce her; and after Lanzhi returned to her own home her brother compelled her to marry again. Finally she drowned herself and her husband hanged himself. Parting from her husband, she said to him:

> *Be your love strong, enduring as the rocks;*
> *Be mine resistant as the creeping vine.*
> *For what is tougher than the creeping vine?*
> *And what more fixed than the eternal rocks?*

These two faithful lovers fell a prey to the feudal marriage system and family system. Indeed this moving tale is a sharp denunciation of the crimes committed in the name of feudal morality, and the husband and wife who resist its cruel conventions to the last are brilliantly and sympathetically drawn. *The Song of Mulan* is another beautiful narrative poem about a girl in the north who disguises herself as a man to take her father's place in the army. When she comes home after a victory poetic licence is used to bring the poem to a dramatic conclusion:

> *Taking off her battle dress*
> *For a maiden's clothes,*
> *She pats her cloudy tresses before the window,*
> *And paints her eyebrows by the mirror.*
> *Then she goes to greet her comrades*
> *And all are amazed—*
> *"Twelve years we were together,*
> *Yet never knew that Mulan was a maid!"*

In a feudal society in which filial piety was considered the supreme virtue and men superior to women, Mulan was a model for all her sex, and the poet has made her a lovable and thoroughly lifelike heroine. Her story, as well as this poem, has been popular for many centuries in China.

About this time there appeared some dramatic dances accompanied by singing. Two famous examples are *The Dancing Maid* and *Prince of Lanling* of the Northern Qi period. The first dance describes a wastrel who ill-treated his young wife, the second a famous warrior who defended his state and loved his men. Though the songs are lost now, the appearance of these dramatic dances indicates the lines along which the classical drama was developing.

The poetry and prose, fiction and drama of the period with which we have just dealt show greater variety than in any preceding dynasty. They give broader and deeper reflection to the social conflicts of the time, and there is greater variety and maturity in literary form. Many writers pandering to the ruling class took a wrong path and produced work devoid of lasting significance; but those who kept close to the people inherited the fine traditions of earlier Chinese literature and succeeded in carrying them forward.

IV. Literature of the Sui, Tang, Song and Yuan Dynasties

The eight hundred years between the end of the sixth century when Emperor Wen Di of Sui united all China to the middle of the fourteenth century when the Yuan dynasty fell form the fourth stage in the history of Chinese classical literature.

The landlord class which had seized political power during the Qin and Han dynasties had now become hereditary landowners; but during the Sui and Tang dynasties fresh economic changes caused their decline, yet another landlord class arose, and there was increased political centralism. The sharp conflict between the landowners and the exploited peasantry remained, while the growing prosperity of handicraft industries and commerce gave birth to an urban class with its own distinctive outlook. Another important feature of this period was the frequent invasion of China by northern tribes, which aroused popular resistance, so that class antagonisms were often interwoven with the struggle for national independence. All these factors had a deep influence on literature.

This whole period can be divided into five shorter ones: the Sui and early Tang dynasties, the later Tang and Five Dynasties, the Northern Song dynasty, the Southern Song and Golden Tartar period, and the Yuan dynasty.

1. Sui and Early Tang Dynasties

We have seen that some literati of the Southern and Northern Dynasties had false values which resulted in a decadent trend in poetry as well as prose. During the Sui dynasty these unhealthy tendencies were overcome, and the works of Yang Su, Xue Daoheng, Li E and others display a new spirit. Early Tang writers, including Wang Ji, Chen Zi'ang and Li Hua, also opposed what was artificial in the literature of preceding dynasties and laid the foundation for a new age in writing.

At the same time some good work was done by those writers still under the old influence, such as Wang Bo, Yang Jiong, Lu Zhaolin and Luo Binwang, commonly known as the "Four Great Poets of Early Tang." They broadened the subject matter of poetry and contributed to the creation of new forms. Thus the *gu shi* or "old style," *lü shi* or "new style" and *jue ju* or "four-lined verse," generally adopted in later classical poetry, originated in this period. The *gu shi* is rather free: the number of lines and words in each line are not fixed, and the rhyming schemes are relatively flexible. Verses of this kind had appeared previously, but this now became a generally accepted form. *Lü Shi* consists of eight lines, *jue ju* of four. These two forms were not new either, but now strict metrical rules were defined for them. By the early Tang dynasty it was established that the second and third couplet in each eight-line verse must be parallelisms. It is generally recognized that the Tang dynasty was the most glorious period in the history of Chinese poetry. By the first half of the eighth century, thanks to the achievements of the early Tang songsters, poetry had reached its full splendour. Among the many outstanding poets of this period the greatest are Du Fu, Li Bai and Wang Wei.

Wang Wei (701-761) was a native of present-day Shanxi. A poet of genius, he was also a brilliant painter and musician. His poems and paintings give such superb expression to the beauty of nature that a later poet, Su Dongpo, said of him: "His poetry is painting, his painting poetry." Here are some

Painting based on one of Wang Wei's poems, by Monk Daoji (1641-?)

examples of his word pictures:

> Leaning on my stick by the gate
> To enjoy the breeze, I hear cicadas at dusk.
> The sun sets beyond the ford,
> From the desolate village rises one plume of smoke . . . .

> The river flows as if it knew men's hearts,
> The birds, as my companions, fly home at dusk;
> A crumbling wall before the ancient ford,
> And autumn hills bathed in the setting sun.

His poems on the countryside round Wangchuan are famous.

Alone I sit in the quiet bamboo glade,
Strike my lyre and cry aloud,
None knows I am here in the forest,
But the bright moon shines on me . . . .

Not a soul on the lonely hillside,
Nothing but voices;
Shadows falling in deep forests
Are reflected on green moss.

With his seemingly simple yet highly polished style he paints scenes which all can see but most men miss, and he is supremely skilful in communicating his mood. His poems give us the same satisfaction as a fine painting.

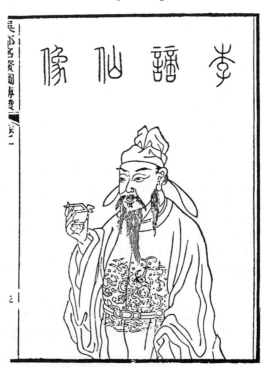

Li Bai, wood-block print dated 1829

Li Bai or Li Taibai was also born in 701. When he was a child his family moved from the north-west to Sichuan, where he grew up. As a man he travelled widely, going to Chang'an in his forties to join the Imperial Academy. When An Lushan's revolt broke out, he became Prince Yong's adviser, but the emperor, fearing this prince might usurp the throne, had him killed and Li Bai exiled to the south-west. Later he was pardoned and returned, to die in 762 in present-day Anhui.

Li Bai was perhaps the most versatile of his generation. He wrote in a variety of poetic forms and styles about many different subjects. Sometimes he imparts to his readers a sense of tranquillity and sheer delight in nature:

> *Gently I stir a white feather fan,*
> *With open shirt sitting in a green wood.*
> *I take off my cap and hang it on a jutting stone;*
> *A wind from the pine trees trickles on my bare head.*

Or:

> *I sat drinking and did not notice the dusk,*
> *Till falling petals filled the folds of my dress.*
> *Drunken I rose and walked to the moonlit stream:*
> *The birds were gone, and men also few.**

He shows a contempt for the nobles and officials who had allowed the country to grow so weak that An Lushan's rebellion nearly overthrew the dynasty. "I was drunk for a whole month, ignoring princes and lords," he wrote once. Again, "How can I stoop to serve the rich and great?" But in spite of his wish to hold aloof from court schemers and place-seekers, he was so far from indifferent to the country's danger that he wrote:

> *I look down at the plain of Loyang*
> *Where the Huns have scattered in flight:*

---

* From *More Translations from the Chinese* by Arthur Waley.

Blood stains the grass; jackals and wolves
Are wearing official caps.

That he knew the sufferings of the people is evident from these lines:

Changan flooded by moonlight
and I in the evening listening
to women from
many homes, pounding clothes
by the water. Chill blows the
autumn wind, ever growing
colder; yet each is anxious
for her lad out at the Yumen Pass
each wondering when we shall
defeat the enemy who drives in
so that he can return and
no longer be a soldier.*

His poems are often exuberantly romantic, but his love of life, generous spirit and closeness to the people make his romanticism healthy and positive.

Du Fu was a native of present-day Henan. He was born in 712 and able to write poems at the age of seven, but failed in all the government examinations. Not till he was over forty did he obtain a low official post. By this time An Lushan's revolt had broken out, and the war and general confusion brought increased hardships to the people. Losing all faith in the government, Du Fu left his post and went to live in Sichuan. He worked for a few years in Chengdu while his friend Yan Wu was governor there. Early in the winter of 770 he died on a boat near Yueyang.

Most of his poems date from after An Lushan's revolt, when the full weakness of the Tang empire was apparent. Du

---

* From *Li Pai: 200 Selected Poems* (Hongkong: Joint Publishing Co., 1980), translated by Rewi Alley.

Du Fu. rubbing from a stone
carving, Qing Dynasty

Fu, with his deep understanding of life and society, wrote poetry more profound than any by his contemporaries. Even before the rebellion he had composed those memorable lines:

> Sour wine and rotting meat
> Behind the red gates of the rich,
> And the road strewn with frozen corpses.
> Great wealth and hunger a few feet apart!

After the rebellion he wrote such immortal poems as "The Xin'an Official" and "The Officer at Tongguan," as well as others dealing with families which had been broken up in those troubled times. A moving example is "The Shihao

Official." ("The Shihhao Official.")

One sunset I came to the village of Shihhao,
And shortly after there followed
An official, seizing conscripts.
In the courtyard of the peasant's house where I stayed,
An old man climbed quickly over the wall, and vanished.

To the door came his old wife to greet the official.
How fiercely he swore at her,
And how bitterly she cried!
"I have had three sons taken
To be soldiers at Yehcheng.
Then came a letter, saying,
Two had been killed, and that the third
Never knew which day he might die.
Now in this hut is left
None but a baby grandson
Whose mother still suckles him. . . .
She cannot go out, as she has no clothes
To cover her nakedness.
All I can do is to go back with you
To the battle at Hoyang.
There I can cook for you,
Even though I am weak and old . . . ."

Night wore on.
The sound of voices died away
until there was left, coming from the hut,
Only the sobbing of the daughter-in-law.
At dawn I rose and left,
With only the old man
*To bid me good-bye.**

Du Fu not only denounced existing evils, but voiced the wish

* Translated by Rewi Alley.

for a better life for all. The following song expresses his profound humanity:

> *Would I had thousands on thousands*
> *Of spacious mansions,*
> *To shelter and gladden all the poor in the world*
> *And protect them from wind and rain.*
> *Ah, if such a building were to appear before me,*
> *Though my own hut fall and I freeze*
> *I should die content!*

His range as a poet is immense. Many of his peoms express faith in mankind's future and ardent patriotism. Others are about his family or friends, some work of art that delights him, or natural beauty. His imagery is strikingly concise:

> *Now for these three months*
> *The beacon fires have flared*
> *Unceasingly*
> *While a letter from home*
> *Is as precious as gold.*
> *And, when I scratch my head,*
> *I find my grey hair grown so sparse*
> *The pin will hold it no more.**

In his later days Du Fu often recalled past incidents and great figures from history to contrast China's former splendour with the decadence of his time, in order to spur his contemporaries on to greater efforts.

> *The Changan of ours today*
> *Becomes like a great*
> *Chessboard, for men*
> *To play with empire; too late*
> *Do we regret the havoc*

* Translated by Rewi Alley.

The ill-spent years have
Wrought; now palaces
And mansions have new lords,
Even the styles of clothing
Change; war drums call
To the northern borders,
Armies are dispatched
To the western region,
Enemies are everywhere; the
Autumn of decadence has
Truly set in, and I feel the chill
Harking back to other times
When things were different. *

Du Fu enlarged the scope of classical poetry, giving it new content and forms. He is generally regarded as the greatest poet of China, with whom none but Qu Yuan can compare.

2. Later Tang and Five Dynasties

From the middle of the eighth century onwards further changes took place in Chinese literature. In prose there was the classical revival, while in poetry there appeared a body of satirical writing of which Bai Juyi was the chief exponent. During this period the development of *ci*, songs with lines of irregular length, and of the short stories known as *zhuan qi* also contributed to the splendour of later Tang literature.

As already indicated, some of the essayists of the Sui and early Tang dynasty modelled their style on the artificial, precious writing of the preceding period, which was condemned by Li E, Li Hua and others. By the time of Han Yu and Liu Zongyuan the tide had turned, and a movement was launched for a "classical revival" in literature.

---

* Translated by Rewi Alley.

Han Yu (768-824) was a native of Nanyang in present-day Henan. Liu Zongyuan (773-819) was a native of Hedong in present-day Shanxi. They held virtually identical views on the reform of prose, and their main aims were: to win greater respect for the Confucian classics, to develop Confucianism, to stress the cultivation of moral qualities, and to learn from the writers of the Warring States Period, Qin and Western Han dynasties. These principles exercised a great influence on Tang essayists and later writers.

Han Yu and Liu Zongyuan put their theories into practice in their own work. Han Yu regarded himself as the exponent of orthodox Confucianism, although he was careful to avoid all archaic figures of speech and expressions dating from the time of Confucius and Mencius. His style is fresh and virile. He once wrote:

> At the start I dared read nothing but works of the Xia, Shang and Zhou dynasties or the Western and Eastern Han dynasties, and dared retain nothing but the precepts of the sages. At rest I seem forgetful and in my actions abstracted, as though lost in thought or bewildered. When I want to express any views, I make a point of dispensing with all outmoded expressions, which is no easy matter.
>
> (From "A Reply to Li Yi")

Liu Zongyuan had the courage to oppose irrational aspects of feudalism, as we can see by his challenge of the succession from father to son which for centuries had determined the system of political control in China.

> The feudal lords today rule by right or primogeniture. But under this system is it true that all those belonging to the hereditary ruling class govern well, while none of those from lower classes do so? If this is not true, who knows what will become of the people!
>
> (From "On Feudalism")

Though Liu Zongyuan had perhaps a less bold style than

Liu Zongyuan, wood-block print dated 1830

Han Yu, he had greater firmness and integrity. Sometimes he used parables to criticize abuses, in such stories as *The Donkey of Guizhou* or *The Rats of Yongzhou.*

In addition to these two great writers, Li Yi, Huangfu Shi, Shen Yazhi and other essayists helped to promote the classical revival, until gradually a new style of prose was created.

In the realm of poetry, the influence of Du Fu made poets adopt a more serious attitude to their work and hold less aloof from politics. The representative poet of this period was Bai Juyi.

Bai Juyi (772-846) was a native of Xiagui in present-day Shaanxi, who started writing poems as a boy and became an official in his twenties. He was banished from the capital several times on account of slander, and served in Jiujiang, Hangzhou, Suzhou and elsewhere, holding fairly important posts towards the end of his life.

A true disciple of Du Fu, Bai Juyi was convinced that literature should combat social evils; and he himself acted on this assumption, for many of his poems are satires. His most famous works are his ten *Shaanxi Songs* and fifty *New Yue Fu*. One of these, "The Old Man with the Broken Arm," denounces the horrors of war:

> *To the north of my village, to the south of my village*
> *   the sound of weeping and wailing,*
> *Children parting from fathers and mothers, husbands*
> *   parting from wives.*
> *Everyone says that in expeditions against the Man tribes*
> *Of a million men who are sent out, not one returns.**

Profound meaning and verbal simplicity characterize these sixty poems, and indeed all Bai Juyi's work. Other poems, simple and spontaneous, reveal his concern for the common people, as in these lines from "The New Silk Jacket":

> *So many go cold and I am unable to help them—*
> *Why should I alone be warm?*
> *My heart knows the peasants' hardships*
> *On farms and in mulberry groves;*
> *My ears ring with the cries*
> *Of the starving and cold.*

Bai Juyi wrote many other fine poems which were not didactic. One of these is his long narrative poem, *Everlasting Remorse*. The love of Emperor Ming Huang for Lady Yang was a theme which appealed to feudal writers, and Bai Juyi's treatment of it in this celebrated poem is superb. He gives

---

* From *170 Chinese Poems*, translated by Arthur Waley.

a powerful description of the emperor's grief after his favourite's death:

On his return the garden was unaltered
With its lotus and its willows;
The lotus recalled her face,
The willows her eyebrows,
And at sight of these
He could not hold back his tears.

At the same time the poet criticized the emperor's former life of sensual pleasure and luxury:

At leisure she danced and sang
To the music of lyres and flutes,
And not for one day would the emperor
Forgo the pleasure of her company
Till battle drums from Yuyang
Caused the earth to quake
And put an end
To the Dance of Feathered Garments.

The revolt of An Lushan in 755 was one of the gravest events in the three hundred years of Tang history and brought untold suffering to the people. In fact, owing to irresponsible government, the dynasty was nearly overthrown.

Although Bai Juyi's sympathies and vision were limited, on the whole he succeeded to a notable degree in expressing his countrymen's inmost thoughts and deepest convictions. He was in the best sense a popular poet.

This was also an age of many lesser poets. Yuan Zhen, Li Shangyin, Du Mu and others, all made their distinctive contribution to Chinese poetry.

In the second half of the Tang dynasty there appeared a new poetic form, the *ci*. *Ci* are lyrics with lines of irregular length set to music. The number of sentences and the number of words in each sentence are governed by definite rules. This form of verse, which had a folk origin, was adopted by poets such as Wen Tingyun of the later Tang dynasty, and Wei Zhuang, Feng Yansi and Li Yu of the Five Dynasties. Of these, Li Yu was the most remarkable. The last prince of the Southern Tang kingdom and a native of Xuzhou in Jiangsu, he lived from 937 to 978. His *ci* deal with days gone by, his old kingdom, his grief and the transience of human life. Though he was far from sharing the feelings of common folk, his keen mind, brilliant imagination, and the beauty and freshness of his language have won him many admirers.

Fiction made rapid strides during the Sui and Tang dynasties, as we can see from a brief survey of the *zhuan qi* or short stories of the Tang dynasty.

The development of the *zhuan qi* can be divided into three periods. The first is from the seventh century and early years of the eighth, when such tales began to be written. Towards the end of the dynasty this genre became popular, and the middle of the eighth century to the early part of the ninth is the second period, when many *zhuan qi* of a high quality were produced. To this time belong the famous *Tale of a Pillow*, *Everlasting Remorse*, *The Story of Yingying*, *The Governor of the Southern Tributary State* and *Prince Huo's Daughter*, as well as collections of tales by one writer. The third period started after the beginning of the ninth century and produced fewer outstanding stories but many collected works. Moreover, as so many such tales were appearing, anthologies were now compiled.

Taken as a whole, these Tang stories, especially those of the second period, give us a vivid and accurate picture of society. *Everlasting Remorse* and *Tale of a Pillow* show the decadent ways and vicious struggle for power of the ruling class. *The Old Man of the East City* and *Red Thread* reflect the horrors of war and the clashes between the different satrapies of that time. *Prince Huo's Daughter*, *The Story of Yingying* and *Fei Yan* describe the unhappy lot of women and their tragic love stories. The characterization and language are magnificent. Most of the writers have a warm, natural style, and by means of significant details bring out the salient features of their characters. We see this in *Prince Huo's Daughter*, the tragedy of a girl whose lover deserts her, when the young man is dragged to her as she lies on her death-bed.

> Jade had been ill so long that she could not even turn in bed without help. But on hearing of his coming, she rose swiftly up, threw on her clothes, and swept out like one possessed.

Similarly in the *Tale of a Pillow*, where Lu dreams that he has been made a high official and then thrown into prison on account of slander, the writer uses intimate touches to convey his hero's bitterness:

> In my old home east of the mountain I had enough good land to keep me from cold and hunger. What possessed me to become an official? See where it has brought me! If only I could put on my fur jacket again, and canter on my black colt down the road to Handan!

By this method these characters are presented to the life—Jade torn between love and hate, and Lu uncertain of his best course of action.

Scholars after the Tang dynasty continued to write *zhuan qi*, but most of these later productions are undistinguished.

The drama showed less advance during this period than fiction, though certain improvements were made on the entertainments popular in the Southern and Northern Dynasties which included acrobatic displays, singing and dancing, puppet shows and burlesques.

3. Northern Song Dynasty

The writers of the Northern Song dynasty carried Chinese

literature another step forward. At the beginning of the Song dynasty, the writers known as the Xikun School sought after formal perfection and took a wrong turning again in their poetry. For a time the *ci* remained fettered by the old conventions of the Five Dynasties, but during the eleventh century writers recovered a more genuine set of values and wrote another glorious chapter in the history of Chinese literature.

The three most prominent men of letters of the eleventh century were Ouyang Xiu, Wang Anshi and Su Shi or Su Dongpo, the last ranking highest.

Ouyang Xiu (1007-1072) was a native of Luling in present-day Jiangxi. Statesman, historian, poet and essayist, he advanced the classical revival initiated during the Tang

Ouyang Xiu

dynasty. His works are lucid and fluent, his style easy and unaffected. One of his essays contains reminiscences of his father told by his mother:

> When your father was an official he sat up by candle-light once over a verdict and kept stopping work to sigh. I asked what the matter was, and he said: "This man is for the condemned cell. I cannot save him." I asked: "Is it right to try?" He answered: "If I try and fail, neither the condemned man nor I need have any regret. And what if there is a chance of succeeding?"

Here in plain, unvarnished language is a graphic picture of a kind-hearted official of those long-past days. Ouyang Xiu also wrote numerous poems in the language of everyday speech and was anxious to act as a spokesman for humble folk, as we see in his "Poem to Du Mo":

> *East of the capital bandits gather;*
> *North of the river new troops are trained;*
> *Each day more hunger and wretchedness*
> *Stalk the roads.*
> *I beg you to raise your voice*
> *On behalf of the people!*

"A Heavy Snowfall" and "Welcome Rain" are among Ouyang Xiu's best works. In prose as well as poetry he served as a model for later generations.

Wang Anshi (1021-1086), famous for his political reforms, was a native of Linchuan in present-day Jiangxi. A minister of state, his literary achievements are inseparable from his radical political proposals. His prose works criticizing social abuses and suggesting reforms go to the heart of the matter and are supremely logical. His language is succinct, his sentences well constructed, his style incisive and lucid. As an example we may quote a passage from his *Reply to Sima Guang*:

> You accuse me, sir, of infringing upon the authority of

other officials, creating trouble, seeking personal profit and refusing advice, thereby causing discontent throughout the empire. To my mind, however, when I receive orders from our sovereign, draw up government statutes and issue them to the authorities, I am not infringing upon the authority of other officials. When I follow the policy of former kings to benefit the people and root out evil, this is not creating trouble. When I regulate the economy of the empire, this is not seeking personal profit. When I combat wrong ideas and refute the sophists, this is not refusing advice. As for the fact that there is much discontent, I knew in advance that this would be the case.

Some of his poetry also is impressive evidence of his concern for the people. Thus "On Contemporary Affairs" is a tragic confirmation of the saying: "Tyranny is worse than a tiger."

> *Heart-stricken in the country,*
> *I grieve for the common people:*
> *Good years cannot fill their bellies;*
> *In flood or drought they must starve;*
> *And if brigands come*
> *How many will lose their lives!*
> *But most I am aghast at the officials*
> *Who ruin nine homes out of ten.*
> *The grain rots in the fields,*
> *But the people have no money to go to court;*
> *If they succeed in approaching an official,*
> *They are beaten for their pains.*

Wang Anshi is also justly celebrated for such nature poems as "Plum Blossom" and "Written on Mr. Huying's Wall," for he was an original thinker with a distinctive style.

Su Shi (1036-1101) was a native of Meishan in present-day Sichuan. He held high office for many years and proved a good, public-spirited official. He was disgraced and demoted several times, being sent on one occasion as far as Hainan Island. His genius was many-sided, for not only was he an immortal poet and prose-writer, but a fine calligrapher and artist.

Su Shi was a careful observer and shrewd judge, who expressed the results of his observation and analysis in clear, flowing language, illumined by brilliant flashes of imagination. Since the end of the Tang dynasty the themes of *ci* had virtually been confined to love or individual joys or sorrows, but at the beginning of the Song dynasty a gradual change came about, most evident in the poems of Liu Yong, whose *ci* are comparatively long and cover a greater range of subjects: the luxury of the capital, the views of townsfolk, the misery and longings of unhappy women, and the experiences of a vagabond life. Su Shi's poetry marks a

"Thought of the Past at Red Cliffs", a Ming illustration (dated 1612) to the poem

further change in style, as can be seen from "Thoughts of the Past at Red Cliff":

> The mighty river flows east,
> Sweeping away countless heroes down the ages;
> An old fortress on the west
> May be Red Cliff where valiant Zhou Yu* fought.
> Jagged rocks scatter foam,
> Fierce billows crash on the shore,
> Hurling up drifts of snow:
> A scene lovely as a painting,
> But how many heroes fell here!
> I think of Zhou Yu that year
> Newly wed to Lord Qiao's daughter,
> Handsome and bold
> With plumed fan and scholar's cap,
> Laughing and joking as his mighty foe
> Was turned to dust and ashes.
> Do you smile at me for a sentimental fool,
> Roaming in spirit through that ancient kingdom
> Though my hair is white before its time?
> Life is but a dream—
> Let me drink a cup to the moon above the river!

This poem pays tribute to an ancient hero and laments the poet's own fate, linking past and present and giving moving expression to the author's sense of affinity with Nature. Su Shi's genius and vast erudition made him deal with a wider range of topics than any other poet, both in his *ci* and other forms of poetry. He took the hardships of the people to heart, writing for instance in the "Lament of a Peasant Woman":

> One month she sleeps on a straw mat in the fields;
> In fine weather she reaps the paddy and carts it home;

* A famous general of the kingdom of Wu in the Three Kingdoms period.

Bathed in sweat, her shoulders aching,
She carries it to market—
To get only the price of bran!
She sells her buffalo to pay her taxes,
Pulls down her house for fuel,
But what can she do next year
To keep from starving?

The poet voices his sympathy for the poor in many of the verses written to friends; elsewhere he expresses his longing to become one with Nature. He has left many short nature poems, much admired for their apt imagery, economy of language and haunting, evocative quality. "The West Lake After Rain," only twenty-eight characters in the original, may be taken as an example of these short lyrics, although it loses its magic in translation:

The brimming lake is a brave sight in the sunlight;
The misty hills have a special charm in the rain:
I would compare the West Lake to Xi Shi*—
Unpainted or made up she was equally lovely.

Su Shi believed that writing should resemble "floating clouds and flowing water." Indeed his prose is swift-moving and spontaneous, showing infinite variety. Sometimes he uses ingenious parables to attack incorrect trends of the time, as in *The Sun*:

One blind from birth has no conception of the sun. If one day he questions someone about the sun, he is told, "The sun is like a brass basin." Then he knocks against a basin and hears it clang, and later takes a bell for the sun. Another man tells him, "The sunlight is like a candle." Then he feels a candle to discover its shape, and later takes

---

* Concubine of the king of Wu in the Spring and Autumn Period. Her beauty is said to have proved her master's undoing.

a flute for the sun. The sun is in fact very different from bells and flutes, but a blind man does not know this because he has never seen it — he goes by hearsay.

Now the Way is more difficult to discern than the sun, and those who do not study are like blind men. So when one who knows the Way speaks of it, even though he is skilled in making apt comparisons he can think of nothing better than a basin or candle; but a basin may make his hearers think of a bell, a candle of a flute, until they get further and further from the truth. Thus when men talk of the Way, they attempt to describe it in terms of what they have seen or to imagine it without having seen it, and in both cases they deviate from the Way.

Su Shi also wrote brilliant essays on historical happenings and current events, as well as on his own feelings and on Nature. He was probably the greatest writer of the Song dynasty, whose works had a lasting influence on later generations.

Li Qingzhao, a poetess who lived towards the end of the Northern Song dynasty, has a special place in Chinese literature.

Li Qingzhao (1081-1145) was a native of Jinan in present-day Shandong. An extremely well-read woman who wrote on many subjects, she is best known for her superb *ci*. She enjoyed several years of happiness after her marriage, and produced fresh, beautiful work. But after fighting broke out towards the end of the dynasty and her husband died, she wrote poignant lines like these to express her loneliness:

> *Faded and withered,*
> *With thinning hair, greying temples,*
> *I have lost the courage to take an evening stroll;*
> *I had best sit by the window*
> *And listen to the laughter and talk*
> *Of others.*

Her sympathies were wide and she was capable of deep

feeling, as is evident from her poems describing conditions in the north after the fall of the dynasty. She is one of China's greatest women writers.

Minor poets of this period were Liu Yong, Zeng Gong, Huang Tingjian and Zhou Bangyan.

4. Southern Song and Golden Tartar Period

The fall of the Northern Song dynasty shook all writers of the time out of their complacency and resulted in an increased variety of subject matter in Southern Song literature. Few masterpieces were produced in this period, but important advances were made in fiction and drama, and

Lu You, wood-block print dated 1856

the foundations were laid to a great extent for the best Yuan, Ming and even Qing writing. From this time onwards fiction and drama occupied increasingly important positions in Chinese literature while poetry and essays took second place.

The patriotic standard-bearers of Southern Song literature were the great writers Lu You and Xin Qiji.

Lu You (1125-1210) was a native of Shanying in present-day Zhejiang. From his boyhood north China's defeat rankled in his heart, and all his life he longed for the recovery of the lost territory. After he became an official he spent ten years in Sichuan, where all the commanders were staunch patriots, and these men encouraged him and influenced his work.

His poems are filled with fervent patriotism. Sometimes he brooded bitterly over China's losses and lashed out at the government for surrendering. He greeted the rare victories with passionate enthusiasm, and even dreamed of the recovery of the north. Thus he wrote:

Towards midnight on the eleventh of the fifth month I dreamed that I accompanied His Majesty on an expedition to reconquer all the territory of the Han and Tang empires. I saw a rich, populous city, and was told this was Xiliang. In raptures, I wrote a poem in the saddle, but woke before it was finished. Now I am completing it.

A million warriors follow the Son of Heaven;
Before his command goes out our land is retaken.
New cities rise at distant frontier stations,
And travelling in state
The emperor proclaims a general amnesty.

Many of his poems reflect his indomitable spirit, but unfortunately he died without seeing China restored to her former splendour. Thus he left his son the heartfelt injunction:

Though I know when a man is dead that is the end,
My one grief is not to have seen this land united.
As soon as our kingly army recovers the north,
Be sure to tell your old man when you sacrifice!*

Lu You's *ci* express the same passion. Thus he wrote:

Now, my hair flecked with white,
I am shocked to find my ambitions come to nothing
And my life that of a wanderer.
A jaded thoroughbred,
Little by little I have lost my mettle;
Far, far away, behind folds of mist and water,
I dream of the mountains and streams of my native
land.

As an ardent patriot, Lu You loved the labourers whose toil supported the country. In his works he prays for good harvests, sighs over the devastation of so many cities, inveighs against the disparity between the rich and the poor, attacks the decadence of the rulers, and shows remarkable respect for the common people's opinions. He was not only with them in spirit, but lived very much as they did, cultivating his land himself.

In midspring a farmer tills his fields
And tends his mulberry trees.
I plant the Lin'an mulberry
To feed hundreds of sheets of silkworms . . . .
South of my lodge I sow sesame,
For three days, luckily, there is no rain,
And getting up the fourth morning
I find the earth already clothed with green.
                    (From "A Country Cottage")

---

* It was the custom, during sacrifice to the ancestors, to announce important family news to their spirits.

In his poems we find detailed descriptions of husbandry and the great satisfaction of those who reap the fruits of their toil. In addition to working himself, Lu You brought up his grandchildren to understand the dignity of labour.

> *My grandsons, late home from school,*
> *With ruffled hair turn to the kitchen garden.*
> *I wish you no rank or riches,*
> *But may you till the land!*
>
> (From "Farming")

Lu You's works combine profound wisdom with beauty of form. His language is fresh and natural, and sometimes he uses colloquialisms. Unhampered by the strict rules of *lü shi*, he wrote many fine poems in this metre about love, friendship and the beauties of Nature. He is undoubtedly one of the greatest Song poets.

Xin Qiji (1140-1207) was a native of Jinan in present-day Shandong. As a young man he fought with the guerrillas against the Golden Tartars, and like Lu You he looked forward all his life to the recapture of China's lost territory. Most of his *ci* breathe a fervent love for his country:

> *When drunk, I trim the lamp to gaze at my sword;*
> *In dreams, I hear bugles sounding from camp to camp.*
> *Meat is sent eight hundred li — the whole length of*
> *the front —*
> *Luting carries across the lines,*
> *As in the field in autumn we train our troops.*

Occasionally in times of great difficulty he fell a prey to despair. He has written poems, too, when intoxicated with the beauty of Nature or the moonlight; but even these are filled with powerful feeling. Indeed his passion for beauty was one expression of his love for his country, which he longed to see powerful and at peace again. His was a versatile genius: he wrote splendid and tragic poems as well as soft, charming lyrics, but his spirit is pre-eminently virile and heroic.

Lesser poets of the Southern Song dynasty include Yang Wanli, Fan Chengda, Chen Liang, Jiang Kui and Wen Tianxiang.

There were not many poets under the Golden Tartars. The most outstanding was Yuan Haowen, a native of Xiurong in present-day Shanxi, who lived from 1190 to 1257. He wrote of the rugged scenery of the north, of his bitterness, of the hardships of the peasants under the invaders, and of the fearful massacres and pillage which took place when the Mongols attacked the country. He describes the agony of countless captives:

> *No cave in the mountain to hide us,*
> *No boat to carry us across the river—*
> *A single enemy horseman*
> *Can take a thousand captives;*
> *And even if we live through this year,*
> *What of the next?*

> *Flight after flight,*
> *Wild geese from south of the river!*
> *Men sing, men weep,*
> *Wild geese lament;*
> *When autumn comes the geese fly back,*
> *But will the captives from the south*
> *Ever see their homes again?*

His deeply moving poems bear certain resemblances to those of Su Shi and Xin Qiji.

Finally we come to the fiction and drama of this period.

The *hua ben* or story-tellers' scripts of this dynasty were used in the pleasure parks in different cities. Story-telling in public places of entertainment started in the Tang dynasty but became more popular during the Song. By and large, these stories dealt with one of three topics: the life of the townsfolk, Buddhist legends, and historical incidents.

Most of the Song and Yuan stories dealing with city life

can be found in such collections as *Popular Tales of the Capital*. Although these stories contain elements of superstition or vulgarity, they deal in the main with the actual society and life of the time. Thus *Fifteen Strings of Cash* describes the ruin of a family of simple townsfolk because a conceited magistrate had no respect for human life. Cui Ning was sentenced to death for murder, despite his pleas that he was innocent.

> In a towering rage, the city magistrate thundered: "Nonsense! How could there be such a coincidence: they lost fifteen strings of cash, and you got fifteen strings for your silk! You are obviously lying. Besides, a man shouldn't covet his neighbour's wife or horse: if she was nothing to you, why were you walking together and putting up together? No doubt a cunning knave like you will never confess until I have you tortured."
>
> . . . The unfortunate concubine and Cui Ning were tortured until they broke down and agreed that they had been tempted by the money and killed Liu, then had taken the fifteen strings of cash and fled. The neighbours, acting as witnesses in the case, put their crosses to the confessions. Cui Ning and the concubine were pilloried and sent to the prison for those condemned to death. And the fifteen strings of cash were returned to Mr. Wang — who found they were not enough to pay the men in the yamen!*

This story, founded on fact, gives us a picture of the crass stupidity, stubbornness and greed of the official world, which meant that the people had no one to defend their rights. Another of these tales, *The Revolt of Wang Xinzhi*, describes a merchant and iron-smelter who built up a fortune by his own efforts but was ruined by the corrupt authorities and forced to take his own life. This man lamented bitterly:

---

* Passages quoted from *Lazy Dragon* (Joint Publishing Co., 1981), translated by Yang Xianyi and Gladys Yang.

I was always a loyal subject till wicked men slandered me and I could not clear myself. I wanted to capture the assistant magistrate, find out the truth, take revenge and wipe out this disgrace. Then I meant to use the money in the local treasury to gather together a band of gallant men, seize the Huai River Valley and sweep away all these grasping, evil officials, to spread my fame throughout the empire. After that I should have placed myself at the service of the state and fought for my country, to win lasting renown. But now I have failed — this is fate!

This sharply delineated hero was a substantial, law-abiding citizen, who was driven by injustice to become an outlaw; and his story enables us to understand the difficulties of his class.

The historical stories which have come down to us in such works as the *Popular History of the Five Dynasties* and *Tales of the Xuan He Period* are the immediate forerunners of the traditional novels. Thus the descriptions of Song Jiang and other peasant leaders given in the *Tales of the Xuan He Period* are the earliest sources for the adventures of the outlaws of Liangshan. This book reflects the unflinching courage and patriotism of common folk, and exposes the pride and extravagance of the rulers and their crimes against the people.

None of the Buddhist story-tellers' scripts have been preserved, but we have a chante-fable describing Xuan Zang's pilgrimage to the west which has certain features in common with both the stories about townsfolk and the historical tales, and is significant because it contains the first account of that immortal figure — Monkey Sun Wukong.

This period saw greater advances in the drama than the Tang dynasty, and the appearance of the long dramatic ballads known as *zhu gong diao* and of the Southern Drama was of particular significance. The dramatic ballads, which contained both songs and recitations, left their mark on the subject matter and music of the Yuan theatre. The Southern

Drama, a form of local opera popular in the coastal regions of Zhejiang from the end of the Northern Song dynasty onwards, may be considered the forerunner of the Ming and Qing plays. Two *zhu gong diao* still in our possession are *Liu Zhiyuan* by an unknown writer of the Song dynasty and *The Western Chamber* by a man named Dong in the Golden Tartar period. Though these are not plays they had a considerable influence on the development of the drama, and the literary merits of *The Western Chamber* are considerable. A fair number of mutilated versions of southern plays dating from the end of the Song and the early Yuan dynasties remain to us. *The Successful Candidate Zhang Xie*, by an unknown writer, is complete. The heroine of this play is a striking figure, and the supporting cast is vividly drawn; the language is simple and concise, sometimes very lively and natural. The influence of this Southern Drama on later plays is obvious.

5. Yuan Dynasty

The main literary achievements of the Yuan dynasty are linked with the northern music. Lyrics set to the northern tunes were known as *san qu*, while the operas which used them were *za ju*, the celebrated Yuan drama. *San qu* are songs with lines of irregular length, somewhat akin to *ci*. Most of the Yuan plays have four acts, occasioanlly more; though if the plot is an involved one, over twenty acts may be used. Apart from *san qu* and plays, this dynasty produced little good literature.

The two greatest dramatists of the Yuan dynasty are Guan Hanqing and Wang Shifu.

Guan Hanqing was a native of Dadu, present-day Beijing. He was probably born at the time of the overthrow of the Golden Tartars, in 1234 or thereabouts, and died at the beginning of the fourteenth century. He had a wider experience of life than most of the literati, and his familiarity with ordinary townsmen enabled him to understand folk art and the life of the man in the street, so that in his work we sense his closeness to the common people.

Guan Hanqing was the most prolific of the Yuan dramatists, and one of the most brilliant. He wrote on a wide range of topics, and the main themes of his plays are positive and clear. No matter whether he is dealing with corrupt officials or petty tyrants, heroes, beautiful girls or talented scholars, all his plays breathe defiant resistance to oppression.

Snow in Midsummer is one of his best works. The central theme of this play is the iniquity of the ruling class, and the main attack is directed against the injustice caused by foolish bureaucrats. The heroine, Dou E (Tou Ngo), has great courage and strength of character. Before her execution she sings:

Illustration to Snow in Midsummer

You think Heaven knows no justice, men no pity?
Almighty Heaven will listen to men's prayers.
Once, in Tunghai, for three years no rain fell,
Because a good daughter-in-law was unjustly treated.
Now your district's turn has come.
Because officers here have no concern for justice.
The common citizens cannot tell the truth!*

The plot is well integrated and highly dramatic, the language simple and moving.

The Butterfly Dream, *The Wife-Snatcher* and *The Riverside Pavilion* show us the overweening pride of the rich and mighty, who could not be called to account for murder and boasted of the fear they inspired. *Rescued by a Coquette*, *Gold Thread Pool* and other plays reflect the sufferings of singsong girls and their fighting spirit. Broad humanity and realism are evident in all these works.

Wang Shifu was a native of Yizhou in present-day Hebei. The exact date of his birth is not known, but he is believed to have been active at the end of the thirteenth and beginning of the fourteenth centuries. After serving for a time as an official, he retired to live as a hermit.

He did not write many plays, and his masterpiece is *The Western Chamber*. Many Yuan dramatists attacked the feudal marriage system under which marriages were determined by money or social position and true love was cruelly suppressed, but *The Western Chamber* is the most outstanding work of this type.

Though the main theme of this play is the love between a scholar named Zhang and Yingying, a girl of good family, the two most striking characters are Yingying and her maid Hong Niang. Yingying's personality was described in some detail in Tang dynasty stories, but Wang Shifu has added finishing touches to it. Hong Niang, however, is entirely his

---

* From *Selected Plays of Kuan Han-ching,* (Shanghai: New Art and Literature Publishing House, 1958), translated by Yang Hsien-yi and Gladys Yang.

Yingying, drawing by Tang Yin (1470-1523)

own creation. Intelligent, lively and brave, she has a strong sense of justice and plenty of fight. When her mistress cross-questions her sternly about the lovers, she gives a confident answer, conscious of being in the right.

Why pry and probe any more, ma'am?
The proverb says: "Grown girls
Should not stay long at home" . . . .
He is a brilliant scholar,
She the most lovely young lady . . . .
If you force her to leave Master Zhang
You will disgrace your house!
She is your own flesh and blood —
Think it over well, ma'am!

Mischievous, ingenious Hong Niang has been a favourite with play-goers down the ages. Another reason for this play's popularity is its masterly construction and its language sparkling with life.

Other plays by Wang Shifu, such as *Beautiful Spring Hall* and *A Tumbledown Cave*, are inferior works.

In addition to Guan Hanqing and Wang Shifu, there were many lesser Yuan dramatists, of whom we may mention two. Bai Pu (1226-1310) was a native of Zhending in present-day Hebei. His best work, *Rain on the Plane Trees*, while dealing with the tragic love of Emperor Ming Huang and Lady Yang, exposes the luxury and licence of the feudal rulers. This play shows penetrating psychological insight, and is skilfully constructed. Ma Zhiyuan, a native of Beijing, lived slightly later than Bai Pu. His most representative work, *Autumn in the Han Palace*, tends to idealize Emperor Yuan of Han, but presents us with a noble heroine in the person of Wang Qiang, contrasting her courage and patriotism with the ineptness and cowardice of the military and civil officials.

A number of stirring Yuan dramas, such as *Distributing Grain at Chenzhou*, are anonymous.

Many Yuan dynasty playwrights, including the four just mentioned, also wrote *san qu*. Other writers who specialized in this genre include Zhang Yanghao, Liu Zhi, Feng Zizhen, Sui Jingchen, Guan Yunshi, Xu Zaisi, and Zhang Kejiu who may be taken as a representative figure.

Zhang Kejiu, a native of Qingyuan in present-day Zhejiang, was probably born in the seventies of the thirteenth century and died in the forties of the fourteenth. He wrote over seven hundred verses, the majority of them dealing with natural beauty, as in this description of Tongbo Mountain in Zhejiang:

> In the pine-scented breeze beside the small pavilion
> A lyre plays a song of immortals.
> The jade hare* shivers in the autumn wind;

---

* Refers to the moon, where the legend says a jade hare lives.

The chilly monkeys wail upon wild branches;
White clouds stretch to the horizon
And the moon is small.

Sometimes he also wrote satires on current abuses:

All men hate poverty,
All delight in riches . . . .
So they paste their essays into purses,
And turn their homes into houses of ill repute!

His language verges occasionally on the pedantic, but he did not deliberately turn his back on common speech.

San qu continued to be written after the Yuan dynasty, becoming, indeed, one of the most popular poetic forms.

The foregoing is necessarily a brief summary only of the literature of the sixth to fourteenth centuries. During this period great poetry and fine essays were written, and unprecedented advances were made in fiction and drama. Owing to the decline of the hereditary landowning class and the growth of large towns and cities, new ideas and subjects were introduced into literature, and new forms and images were created. These factors combined with the development of the Chinese language to make these eight hundred years a fruitful period in the history of Chinese literature.

V. Literature of the Ming and Qing Dynasties

The fifth stage in the history of Chinese literature is from 1368, when the Ming dynasty was founded, to the Opium War of 1840.

This period saw a further expansion of manufactures and commerce, there was a great variety of handicraft industries, and in some of these machinery began to be introduced, while trade, both foreign and domestic, increased to a degree hitherto unknown. These developments contributed to the growth of capitalist elements in the economy. The dynastic rule of this period, however, was marked by an unprecedented degree of centralization and political absolutism. At the same time there was a further deterioration in the examination system, and the stereotyped *bagu* essay which was required of all candidates fettered independent thought. But under the influence of nascent capitalism, there was a steady growth of democratic ideas, accompanied by a new flowering of literature.

As the works of this stage underwent great changes, we may for convenience divide it into three periods: early Ming, later Ming, and from the beginning of the Qing dynasty to the Opium War.

1. Early Ming Dynasty

Early Ming literature, and notably drama and fiction,

developed further from the standard reached in the Song and Yuan dynasties.

The *za ju* continued the traditions of the Yuan drama, while the Southern Drama made new progress and produced such famous long operas as *The Tale of the Lute*. These operas set to southern music were known as *zhuan qi*.

Gao Zecheng, the author of *The Tale of the Lute*, was a native of Yongjia in present-day Zhejiang, who was born early in the fourteenth century and died in its seventies. Conventional in his outlook, he believed that the theatre should help to uphold feudal morality. He had a sense of justice too, however, and was able to give a realistic picture of the truth, so that the impact of *The Tale of the Lute* on those who see it is not what its author intended. By contrasting the poor and the rich he has shown us the real society of his time: the pride and extravagance of great officials and landowners are contrasted with the sufferings of the people whom they oppressed so cruelly. Of the principal characters, Miss Niu, Cai Yong's second wife, is relatively insipid and weak; but Cai Yong's vacillation is most strikingly presented, and his first wife, Zhao Wuniang, is even more brilliantly depicted. In the scene "Feeding on Husks," her selflessness and nobility of character are powerfully brought out. During her husband's absence, she is alone to look after his parents, but because there is a famine she can feed them only by eating husks herself.

> *The tears roll down my cheeks;*
> *My heart is a tangled skein;*
> *My legs will barely support me —*
> *What fearful times are these!*
> *Unless I eat these husks*
> *I cannot stay my hunger,*
> *But how can I swallow husks?*
> *I had better die before them*
> *That I may not know when they perish.*
> *I can see no hope —*
> *Nothing can save us!*

Her mother-in-law, who suspects her of eating well in secret, sheds tears when she finds Wuniang trying to swallow husks, and the great merit of *The Tale of the Lute* is that readers or spectators are equally moved. The play's virtues far outweigh its shortcomings.

Four other famous plays of this time are Zhu Quan's *The Thorn Hairpin*, *The White Rabbit* (or *Liu Zhiyuan*) by an unknown author, *The Secluded Chamber* (or *Praying to the Moon*) attributed to Shi Hui, and *Death of a Dog* attributed to Xu Zhen. All these plays have a positive message, for they praise constant lovers, attack arranged marriages and the crimes of landowners and tyrants, and preach brotherly love.

The novels written at the beginning of the Ming dynasty developed from the story-tellers' scripts of the Song and Yuan dynasties. The most important are the *Outlaws of the Marsh* and the *Romance of the Three Kingdoms*.

Outlaws of the Marsh describes the heroic exploits of the peasant army led by Song Jiang during the Northern Song dynasty. Their adventures had been related in the story-tellers' script *Tales of the Xuan He Period*; but this story, improved on by countless folk artists, is believed to have been recast by the great writer Shi Nai'an, who made of it a profoundly-significant and beautiful classic. Shi Nai'an was a native of Baiju in present-day Jiangsu, who lived from approximately 1296 to 1370. His version of the *Outlaws* was further modified by later authors — sometimes to its detriment.

There are a hundred and eight brave men in this epic novel. The majority are peasants, fishermen or other working folk, but some are small functionaries, army officers, merchants, scholars or even landowners persecuted by the higher authorities. They are all robust characters with a strong sense of justice and tremendous courage, capable of fighting to the death, and able to distinguish clearly between right and wrong, friend and foe. Yet in depicting all these outlaws, the author has made each a sharply defined individual. Song Jiang, Wu Yong and the other leaders in Liangshan have widely differing temperaments. Song Jiang is shrewd and experienced, generous and just, and so great is his fame that men are glad to serve him. At first he respects and upholds the feudal order, but gradually his views change, and he determines to revolt. In the mountains his wise strategy enables the outlaws to build up a strong rebel force, until finally he is taken in by an imperial amnesty which destroys the political power the peasants are beginning to establish. The novel gives a detailed description of his reaction to this amnesty. Wu Yong is the strategist of the peasant army, a wily tactician whose sagacity enables him to win a series of victories. It is he who helps to secure Liangshan as the rebel base, who devises brilliant tactics for battles and sometimes settles disputes between different commanders. He is willing to compromise when the amnesty is declared, but when Song Jiang dies he kills himself before his leader's grave. There are many other striking figures in this book like Li Kui, Wu Song and Lu Zhishen. Li Kui is a true peasant, simple, blunt, generous and sincere. He is every inch a rebel, completely loyal to his fellows and with an inveterate hatred for the enemy; but his simplicity is mixed with coarseness. Wu Song is a man of iron, of stupendous strength and courage, who burns to avenge himself once his illusions about the ruling class are shattered. Lu Zhishen is another incomparable fighter, hot-headed, trusty, a champion of the weak, who is hounded into joining the peasant army. The author's characterization is so superb that to this day Song Jiang, Li Kui and these other heroes still live in the hearts of millions.

In addition to brilliant characterization, the *Outlaws* presents us with many unforgettable scenes like "The Gift Is Taken by Guile," "Storming Daming City," "The Three Attacks on Zhu Family Village," "Lu Zhishen Spreads Havoc on Mount Wutai," "Lin Chong Ascends the Mountain One Snowy Night," and "Wu Song Kills the Tiger on Jingyang Ridge." The episode known as "The Gift Is Taken by Guile," for instance, describes how a grasping, dishonest official sends guards to escort his gift to the eastern capital, and how Chao Gai and seven other stout fellows pretend to be merchants in order to seize this ill-gotten treasure. One blazing hot summer day as the guards are toiling up the mountain, the eighth rogue, Bai Sheng, appears too.

In less time than it takes to eat half a bowl of rice, another man appeared in the distance. Carrying two buckets on the ends of a shoulder-pole, he sang as he mounted the ridge:

> *Beneath a red sun that burns like fire,*
> *Half scorched in the fields is the grain.*
> *Poor peasant hearts with worry are scalded,*
> *While the rich themselves idly fan!*

Still singing, he walked to the edge of the pine grove,

"The Gift Is Taken by Guile", from a Ming edition of Outlaws of the Marsh

rested his buckets and sat down in the shade of a tree.
(Chapter 16.)*

After a battle of wits, the drugged wine takes effect on the
escort, and the outlaws are able to seize the treasure. In this
episode the author indicates the ingenuity and cunning of Wu
Yong and the rebels, while Bai Sheng's short song epitomizes
the gulf between rich and poor.

The *Romance of the Three Kingdoms* is ascribed to Luo
Guanzhong, who is believed to have based it on material in
story-tellers' scripts. Luo Guanzhong was a native of
Qiantang (some say of Taiyuan), who is thought to have
lived during the last seventy years of the fourteenth century.
His work was retouched by later writers.

This novel has as its background the stirring and troubled
times during the third century when China was divided into
three kingdoms. It shows us the open clashes and secret
feuds between different political groups, and the popular
estimate of the chief figures of the time. Liu Bei is presented
as a leader who loves the people, while Guan Yu and Zhang
Fei are heroes who have so captured readers' imagination that
"The Compact in the Peach Orchard," which describes how
they became Liu Bei's sworn brothers, is familiar to every
Chinese household. Zhuge Liang is the personification of
shrewdness and intelligence, a penetrating observer of life, a
man of remarkable judgement, who adapts himself skilfully
to sudden changes. He longs to make the country secure. He
is tolerant and magnanimous, careful and responsible in all
he does, and his accurate foresight in matters great as well
as small is particularly striking. The first time he meets Liu
Bei they discuss the state of the country:

Liu Bei said: "Sir, your statesmanship is amazing.
How can you spend your whole life buried in the country?

---

* From Sidney Shapiro's translation, *Outlaws of the Marsh* (Foreign Languages
Press, 1980).

Have compassion on men, I beg you, and remove my ignorance by your instruction."

Zhuge Liang smiled and said: "What is your ambition, general?"

Liu Bei sent the others out, moved closer and answered: "The house of Han is toppling, evil ministers have usurped authority. Weak as I am, I desire to restore good rule throughout the realm; but my understanding is so limited that I do not know how to achieve this. If you, sir, will lighten my darkness and save me from taking false steps, I shall be inexpressibly grateful!" (Chapter 38.)

Zhuge Liang meets Liu Bei, from an early Qing edition of Romance of the Three Kingdoms

Then follows the scene famed in history when Zhuge Liang gives Liu Bei a detailed summary of the situation in the country, pointing out that it will not be easy to destroy Cao Cao or Sun Quan, his two chief rivals, unless two lesser chieftains are first defeated.

Zhuge Liang paused to order his boy to fetch a map, and when this was hung on the wall he pointed at it. "There are the fifty-four districts of Sichuan," he said. "To win supremacy, general, you must let Cao Cao keep the north and Sun Quan the south; but you can triumph by winning over the people. First take Jingzhou as your headquarters, and then build up a base in the west. Once you are strongly entrenched in these three places you can make plans to conquer the whole empire."

When Liu Bei heard this he rose and bowed with clasped hands, saying: "Your words, sir, have swept away the clouds for me and let me see the clear sky . . . ."

So in this one conversation, Zhuge Liang, who had never left his cottage, foresaw the three parts into which the empire would be divided. Indeed, his equal could not be found in all history! (Chapter 38.)

Here the author not only reveals how eagerly Liu Bei sought for men of talent, but gives us a graphic picture of the countryman who was to become such a brilliant statesman and strategist. Cao Cao is painted, by way of contrast, as a thoroughgoing villain.

In brief, the *Romance of the Three Kingdoms* is a vast canvas depicting the struggle between different factions during that period of feudalism, and subtly voicing the people's aspirations. This classic has had an immense and lasting influence on subsequent generations. If it has its weaknesses, they are in the choice of certain historical episodes and the relative prosiness of the language.

We come now to the essays and poetry of the early Ming dynasty.

The literature of this period developed during a clash

between opposing schools. The "classical language" evolved during the Tang and Song dynasties had by degrees become so corrupted that many writers were studying the prose of the Zhou, Qin and Western Han dynasties to correct the current shortcomings. This school is represented by the "Early Seven," headed by Li Mengyang and He Jingming, and the "Later Seven," headed by Li Panlong and Wang Shizhen. In the realm of poetry, they took the best Tang poets as their models. Though there is an air of spurious antiquity about some of their works, most of these writers had a sense of justice and were in touch with the life of the time. Thus Li Panlong in his *Farewell to Zhang Boshou, County Tutor of Ningjin* sheds light on the bureaucratic system of government.

> High officials today dare undertake nothing of advantage to the state; their subordinates have too many scruples and lack enterprise; while the lowest of all can make no use of their limited intelligence. Even talented officers remain mere bureaucrats, buried in their offices and a slave to their public stipend.

Gui Youguang, Tang Shunzhi and others opposed those who imitated the Qin and Han prose, and were in favour of adopting the spirit of Han Yu and Liu Zongyuan instead. They argued that language should be simple and clear; and Gui Youguang's essays in particular are popular. Gui Youguang (1506-1571) was a native of Kunshan in Jiangsu, who used homely language to describe daily life, as in *The Death of Cold Blossom:*

> The maid who was part of my wife's dowry died on the fourth day of the fifth month of the Ding You year of the Jia Jing era,* and was buried in the country. Fate would not let her serve us any longer! She was ten when she

* A.D. 1537.

entered our service, had two braids and was wearing a dark green dress. One day when it was cold she lit a fire to cook water-chestnuts, filling a small basin with them; but when I came in from outside and asked for some she would not give me any, and my wife laughed at her. Whenever my wife ordered her to eat by our table, she obeyed, rolling her eyes, and my wife would tease her. But all this was ten years ago. Ah, the pity of it!

The prose of Tang Shunzhi and Gui Youguang was influenced by the *bagu* essay, however, which imposed limitations in it.

Some early Ming writers of *san qu* deserve attention, especially Wang Pan and Feng Weimin. Wang Pan was a native of Gaoyou in Jiangsu, who was probably born in the middle of the fifteenth century and died at the beginning of the sixteenth. He loved to make trips into the country, and wrote enchanting descriptions of the beauties of Nature:

> *The grazing cattle are dotted over the plain;*
> *The night is as bright as daylight.*
> *We lodge this evening under the vault of heaven,*
> *Wrapped in our fishermen's capes beneath the stars.*

Not all his poems are idyllic, however, for he wrote many lines such as these:

> *Gongs sound for the festival,*
> *But a thousand households are sad,*
> *A thousand lament.*
>
> (From "The Lantern Festival")

In such poems as "A Great Snowfall" we see how he hated the forces of reaction which "sowed suffering throughout the land."

Feng Weimin (1511-1580?) was a native of Linqu in Shandong. As a young man he endeavoured to be a good official, but since the political conditions would not permit this he was finally forced to resign from his post. He wrote over four hundred *san qu*, most of them rich in social significance. Thus "Retiring from Office" sheds light on the law courts of the time:

> *Whoever offends him comes to grief at once,*
> *Whoever angers him is ruined the selfsame day;*
> *Just, law-abiding citizens cannot escape;*
> *Those who love their country and people are struck down —*
> *Where is there any justice?*

Corruption revolted him, and in his satire "Heaven and Hell" he describes bribery as something pertaining to hell.

> *Those with money must bring it quickly;*
> *Those with none need not be alarmed:*
> *There are other ways to have your sentence repealed.*
> *Give me a gold or silver brick for my bridge,*
> *Oil for the vats by my stove,*
> *Or some sticks of wood or charcoal to heat my kang.*
> *If you cannot redeem yourself so,*
> *Give me that coat you have on!*

Feng Weimin took a great interest in rural life and in farming. Once he celebrated the fall of timely rain in a verse:

> *They're all out, the pea and bean flowers,*
> *And under the trellis golden gourds are swelling.*
> (From "Seasonable Rain")

Few writers have identified themselves so completely with the peasants as Feng Weimin, whose language is also taken from common speech and is lively, fresh and concise. His long poems are well constructed, logically reasoned and full of spirit. All these factors contributed to make his a distinctively virile style.

2. Later Ming Dyansty

Towards the middle of the sixteenth century a change gradually took place in Chinese literature, although of course no hard and fast line of demarcation exists. Thus whereas Gui Youguang and Feng Weimin show a close affinity to the writers of the Song and Yuan dynasties, there are more new elements in the works of Wu Cheng'en and Xu Wei. This change coincided with fresh developments in the drama; and the excellent lyrics and stories which appeared during the second half of the dynasty made this a flourishing period for literature.

The novels of the early Ming dynasty, including *Outlaws of the Marsh* and the *Romance of the Three Kingdoms*, had developed from the historical tales of the Song and Yuan dynasties, and were often the work of more than one man. This was not the case with *The Pilgrimage to the West* and *Jin Ping Mei*. Although the source material of *The Pilgrimage to the West* dates from much earlier, this novel is by and large the work of one man — Wu Cheng'en; and despite the fact that we do not know the identity of the author of the *Jin Ping Mei*, there is a big difference between this book and the story-tellers' scripts.

Wu Cheng'en (c. 1500-1580) was a native of Huai'an in Jiangsu, who came of a family in modest circumstances and failed to distinguish himself in his official career. He retired in later life to devote himself to writing.

His most popular work is *The Pilgrimage to the West*, which drew largely on earlier Buddhist legends about Xuan Zang's adventures and the Yuan and Ming plays based on these. Although this story is full of spirits and monsters, the author has made of it an epic of the human spirit and man's stubborn resistance to all the powers of darkness. For Monkey Sun Wukong is intensely human. Romantically conceived and brilliantly executed, he personifies the Chinese people's struggle against difficulties and defiance of feudal authority. In Chapter 7, when Monkey is creating havoc in

Illustration from an old edition of Pilgrimage
to the West *published about 1635*

heaven, he sings to the Buddha:

> *The Heavenly Palace will not be theirs for ever,*
> *On earth kingdoms rise and fall;*
> *The strongest will prevail,*
> *And heroes will contend for supremacy here.*

He also says:

> Though he has been here since childhood, he can't
> expect to have this place to himself for ever. The proverb
> says: "Emperors come and go, and next year it will be our
> turn." Just tell him to move out and leave heaven to me.

If he won't I shall make so much trouble he will not have a moment's peace! (Chapter 7.)

After Monkey has helped to obtain the scriptures, his courage and perseverance in the face of enormous odds are even more evident. A wily, fearless fighter but kind and loyal friend, he radiates optimism and humour. He is undoubtedly one of the most popular figures in all Chinese literature.

Pigsy and Xuan Zang are well portrayed too. Though Pigsy is stupid, careless, greedy and lecherous, he is simple and honest and sticks to his friends till they have procured the scriptures, leaving readers with an amused affection for him. Xuan Zang was a historical figure, and the author has succeeded admirably in expressing his determination to overcome difficulties as well as his kindliness and sincerity, although sometimes he seems a little stiff and pedantic.

In the course of presenting these characters, Wu Cheng'en exposes the sharp contradictions in the society of the time, the rulers' suppression of all rebels, the corruption of the government and stupidity and greed of the officials. Stringent social criticism and satire are interwoven with humour in this immortal classic.

The *Jin Ping Mei* is believed to have been written by a native of Shandong who lived during the sixteenth and seventeenth centuries. The chief character, Simen Qing, is a merchant of Qinghe, and through the story of his household this novel gives us a picture of many aspects of society. We see the enterprise of the merchants of the Ming dynasty, the relationships between the townsfolk and other classes, and the decadence and cruelty of the rich and powerful. Simen Qing is drawn to the life — an unscrupulous rake who has made a fortune through commerce and usury. All the women have marked individual traits, Golden Lotus in particular. Wu Yueniang is simple and weak, Li Ping'er circumspect, and Golden Lotus a spitfire fond of intrigue. Unfortunately this magnificent work is marred by pornographic passages.

These two classics and the earlier *Outlaws of the Marsh* and *Romance of the Three Kingdoms* are the four great novels of

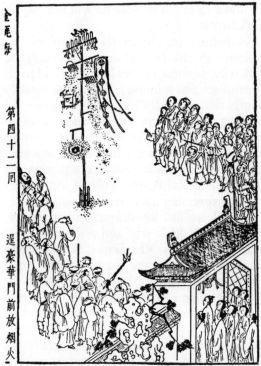

A fireworks show, from an old edition of Jin Ping
Mei published between 1629-1643

the Ming dynasty.

Ming playwrights carried forward the traditions of the
Yuan dynasty. Most of the earlier dramas had been based on
folk legends, and if these were unfamiliar or unacceptable to
the general public the author changed certain episodes or
characters to suit the popular taste. The contents of most of
the later plays, however, were of interest only to scholars.
The themes changed, and with them the ideas expressed.
Considerable independence of thought was shown. Indeed,
we often find fun poked at the time-honoured concept of
sage rulers and worthy ministers. There are modifications
too in the form, language and music, which become more
marked towards the end of the dynasty. The chief play-

wrights of this period were Xu Wei, Ye Xianzu, Chen Yujiao and Meng Chengshun.

Xu Wei, the most outstanding, was a native of present-day Shaoxing in Zhejiang, who lived from 1521 to 1593. The growth of democratic ideas in China is very evident in his plays, which oppose feudal traditions, emphasize the importance of individuality and demand emancipation. His works include *The Story of Mulan*, *The Successful Woman Candidate* and other plays remarkable for their strong spirit of revolt. They ridicule cruel, avaricious officials and the prudish, rigid rules of the monasteries, and show sympathy for women of ability and scholars persecuted for resisting the authorities. The dialogue is vivid, realistic and spirited. Though not entirely the language of common speech, it is a distinctive style achieved by the author after years of hard work. Xu Wei ignored many of the conventions regarding musical accompaniment and form, and his plots are weak because his plays are primarily dramatic poems.

After the middle of the Ming dynasty the *zhuan qi* underwent changes too. Folk-tales ceased to be the main subject matter, and the authors often chose their themes from history or comtemporary life. The best-known dramatists were Liang Chenyu, Shen Jing, Tang Xianzu, Gao Lian, Sun Renru and Li Yu, of whom Tang Xianzu and Li Yu hold the highest place.

Tang Xianzu (1550-1617) was a native of Linchuan in Jianxi, and a courageous official who was not afraid to offend the powerful and noble. He was influenced by the democratic ideas of the time. His chief works are *The Governor of the Southern Tributary State*, *The Purple Hairpin* and *The Peony Pavilion*.

The Peony Pavilion, his greatest work, is an attack on feudal morality in which Tang Xianzu reveals the harm done by the feudal family education and extols love which is stronger than death. His heroine Du Liniang is a significant character, for she represents all the girls deprived of love and happiness. She sings with feeling:

What a riot of brilliant purple and tender crimson
Among the ruined wells and crumbling walls!
What an enchanting sight on this fine morning —
But who takes delight in the spring? . . .
Clouds drift and flutter down at dawn and dusk
Over the green pavilion and painted barges,
Across the misty waves in wind and rain;
But those behind silk screens
Make light of this fine season.

(From "The Girl's Dream")

Because her lament for the spring, which was in fact a lament for herself, expressed the feelings of thousands like her, she became one of the best-loved heroines in the classical theatre. Her story has inspired countless readers, especially young people, and given them the courage to fight for their happiness. The effectiveness of this play owes much to the beauty and freshness of the language.

Tang Xianzu's other works, while inferior to *The Peony Pavilion*, breathe the same spirit of revolt. At the heart of his descriptions of immortals, ghosts and dreams is an intense hatred for social injustice, and this accounts for the rich vein of satire in his works.

Li Yu (1590-1660?) was a native of Suzhou. He wrote over thirty works, the foremost of which is *The Loyal Citizens.* This play describes the resourcefulness and courage of the citizens of Suzhou and their allies in their tussle with the wicked Wei Zhongxian and his henchmen at the end of the Ming dynasty. In spirited terms, the author describes the people's wrath:

The fury spreading from Suzhou over the country
Is unparalleled in history.
The public indignation cannot be curbed;
Nothing can check it now.
Though the officials are fierce as wolves and tigers,
The people's roar for justice
Has shaken heaven and earth;

Soon dark clouds will be swept away!

As Li Yu was over thirty at the time of this riot, he may well have taken part in it himself. *Fighting Against Taxation* deals with the mass resistance to taxation in 1601 in Suzhou. These are some of the finest *zhuan qi* of the Ming dynasty. They deal with the most burning topics of the day, and champion the cause of justice.

Mention should also be made of such later Ming writers as Yuan Hongdao, who opposed the imitation of the old, the songs, fiddle ballads and drum ballads popular among the people, and the tales written in the style of the story-tellers' scripts.

The slavish imitation of the ancients popular in the period before this now aroused the opposition of many scholars, notably of the three brothers Yuan Zongdao, Yuan Hongdao and Yuan Zhongdao. Influenced by the democratic thought of the time, they opposed taking the old classical writers as models and strongly condemned the use of ancient phrases, believing that a writer should cultivate his own individual style. They express independent ideas and unrestrained emotions in frank and natural language.

> They sit in dung heaps chewing offal and relay on powerful patrons to bully honest folk, like most family retainers in Suzhou today. Remembering a few stale anecdotes, they boast of their great learning; using one or two *clichés*, they call themselves poets. (Yuan Hongdao's *Letter to a Friend*.)

This is a merciless blast at the plagiarists of the time! As some of these works were empty or vulgar, Zhong Xing, Tan Yuanchun and others advocated the use of far-fetched expressions to remedy these defects, but since this was not an ideal solution, their writing too had a good many short-comings. Only Zhang Dai succeeded in combining the best features of the two schools. When China was overrun by the

Manchus he suffered many hardships and lived deep in the mountains. He has left us *Reminiscences of Tao An* and other works.

The *xiao qu* of the Ming dynasty are the popular songs belonging neither to the Southern nor the Northern Music, most of which were composed by folk artists. As the people loved them, they spread very widely. Most of them deal with simple, honest love, or describe the sufferings of constant lovers:

> *Dew-drops like pearls upon the lotus leaves —*
> *In my folly I long to thread them!*
> *You are inconstant as water*
> *Which flows off and back again;*
> *My cruel, faithless lover,*
> *You chop and change with the wind!*

A characteristic of these songs is their simple intimate language. Scholars of the time who studied them were able to a certain extent to overcome the growing artificiality of *san qu*.

The drum ballads and fiddle ballads were a combination of recitation and singing. The drum ballads were popular in the north, the fiddle ballads in the south. One of the best examples of the latter is the *Ballad of Twenty-one Dynasties* by Yang Shen. There are many good drum ballads too. The *Ballad of Times Past* by Jia Yingchong casts doubt on the orthodox interpretation of history, and refutes some of the lies of the ruling class. Gui Zhuang at the end of the Ming and beginning of the Qing dynasty wrote a work akin to drum ballads called *Eternal Sorrow* to extol the overthrow of the Mongol dynasty and rebuke the traitors who sold their country to the Manchus. He also pours scorn on "sages and worthies," including Confucius and Mencius.

> *How ridiculous that that old scribbler Confucius*
> *Should keep harping back to bones already dead*
> *Two hundred and forty years before!*

And stranger still that that old wrangler Mencius
Should keep trying to impress men
With the Five Emperors and Three Kings!

Thanks to its advanced ideas, vivid language and pleasant music, this work remained popular for many years.

Last of all there are the stories in the vernacular.

Whereas the earlier story-tellers' scripts deal largely with daily life, Buddhist legends or history, most of those by Ming dynasty writers describe ordinary men and women. During the later half of the dynasty a number of collections appeared, notably *Tales of Qing Ping Hermitage*, *Stories to Teach Men*, *Stories to Warn Men* and *Stories to Awaken Men*, which contained many works of a high quality. Some of them, it is true, border on the fantastic like certain of the Song and Yuan stories; but for the most part they deal with everyday life. Thus *The Pearl Vest* and *The Tangerines and the Tortoise Shell* are concerned with merchants; *The Proud Scholar* and *A Prefectship Bought and Lost* are a scathing reflection on political corruption; while some of the most dramatic deal with the fate of women, as in the case of *The Beggar Chief's Daughter*, *The Oil Vendor and the Courtesan* and *The Courtesan's Jewel Box*. The beggar chief's daughter and the courtesan Decima have inconstant lovers, and the beautiful Flower Queen alone has a happy marriage with the honest oil vendor Qin Zhong. These tales depend for their success upon their dramatic plots and the human interest of the fresh, detailed narrative which is so true to life.

3. Qing Dynasty

After the middle of the seventeenth century there were few essayists or poets of the first rank, but this was the great age of the novel and drama. The masterpieces of this period were: *Strange Tales of Liaozhai* by Pu Songling, *The Palace of Eternal Youth* by Hong Sheng, *Peach Blossom Fan* by Kong Shangren, *The Scholars* by Wu Jingzi and *A Dream of Red Mansions* by Cao Xueqin.

Pu Songling (1640-1715) was a native of Zichuan in Shandong, who met with little success in the state examinations and remained a private tutor all his life. He is the author of many works, best known for his *Strange Tales of Liaozhai.*

The *Strange Tales of Liaozhai* takes its material from stories about ghosts and supernatural beings, as well as the amazing adventures of men. Through these tales Pu Songling satirized rapacious officials, denounced the examination system, showed his sympathy for the sufferings of the people and the hard lot of women, and applauded true love and

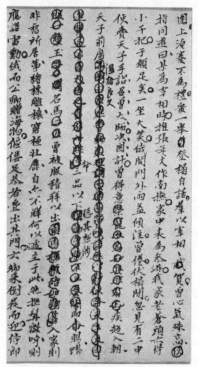

Manuscript of Strange Tales of
Liaozhai

the defiance of convention. Some of his best stories are *The Cricket*, *Wang Zi'an*, *Lian Cheng*, *The Chrysanthemum Spirit*, *Madam Zhou* and *The Dream of the Wolf*. *The Cricket* deals with a time when high officials liked to keep fighting crickets and forced their subordinates to find good specimens for them. When a minor functionary failed to produce a good fighter he was cruelly beaten; so when he finally produced a champion he put it away carefully, meaning to present it to his superior.

When his nine-year-old son saw the father was out, he uncovered the pot on the sly. At once the cricket jumped out and sprang about so nimbly that it eluded his graps. He finally grabbed it, but in doing so pulled its legs off and crushed it so that soon after it died. Then the frightened boy ran crying to his mother, and when she heard what had happened her face turned deadly pale.

"You young rascal! You'll be in trouble when your father comes home!"
The child went off in tears.

Soon the father came back, and when he heard his wife's story he felt as if he had been turned to ice. In a passion he searched for his son, who was nowhere to be found until at last they discovered his body in the well. The father's anger then changed to grief. He groaned and longed to kill himself. Husband and wife sat in their thatched and smokeless cottage facing each other in silence, at their wit's end.

In this story the boy's spirit takes the form of a cricket, and after his father presents this to his superior it proves such a good fighter that all the officials through whose hands it passes are promoted and make their fortune, even the father being rewarded. Pu Songling gives a lively description of how crickets are caught and how they fight, incidentally painting a graphic picture of the misery of the common people and the capriciousness of the officials upon whose whims their well-being depends. Though the story contains elements of the supernatural, it has deep significance and emotional appeal.

Pu Songling also wrote some popular ballads in simple humorous language, dealing with political and household affairs. His writing is realistic, and his characters are full of vitality.

The chief dramatists of the Qing dynasty were Li Yu, Hong Sheng, Kong Shangren and Jiang Shiquan, of whom Hong Sheng and Kong Shangren were the greatest. Hong Sheng (1645-1704) was a native of Hangzhou. His masterpiece, *The Palace of Eternal Youth,** deals with the story of Emperor Ming Huang of the Tang dynasty and Lady Yang. He sings of the love which triumphs over death:

> *True lovers are immortal;*
> *Thus, though the fairy mountain is far away,*
> *True love can reach it.*
> *Love transcends life and death,*
> *And lovers will meet at last . . . .*
>
> (From "The Lovers' Reunion")

He also lays a grave charge against place-seekers and officials.

> *Courtiers and ministers*
> *Have learned a new servility,*
> *Flocking to fawn on the mighty*
> *As country folk flock to a fair . . . .*
> *Yet none dare tell the emperor*
> *That these vermilion roofs and brilliant tiles*
> *Are stained with the people's blood!*
>
> (From "The Writing on the Wall")

---

* Published in English by Foreign Languages Press, 1955. Translated by Yang Hsien-yi and Gladys Yang.

As the characters in this opera are from all walks of life, it gives us a colourful pageant of Tang history. The plot is superbly constructed in the main, the imagery is fresh and beautiful, and the music is delightful; but the dramatic effect of the whole is weakened by certain superfluous episodes in the second half which the author inserted in order to bring Lady Yang and the emperor together in paradise.

Kong Shangren (1648-1718) was a native of Qufu in Shandong. He lived in relatively straitened circumstances, and while working on water conservancy came into fairly close touch with the labouring people. His major work is *Peach Blossom Fan*, and he also collaborated with Gu Cai on *The Smaller Lute.*

Peach Blossom Fan portrays the harrowing events at the time of the fall of the Ming dynasty. The love story of a scholar and a courtesan is used to reveal the reasons for China's defeat, the chief of which was, in the author's opinion, the despicable selfishness of great officials and landowners, who ground down the people, persecuted honest men, and sold the country to the Manchus. The scene "In the Prison" sheds light on the injustice and confusion of those times:

> *Moonlight floods the azure sky,*
> *Heart-rending groans full the air;*
> *New ghosts in the corners of the cells*
> *Complain, dripping with blood . . . .*
> *The dungeon is filled with wailing,*
> *And fetters clank at night . . . .*
> *Do not look down on learning:*
> *All the best scholars*
> *Must undergo tribulation . . . .*
> *These prison cells*
> *Are filled with academicians.*

By this means Kong Shangren exposes the chaos in the government, and the way in which traitors persecute genuine patriots. It is quite clear on which side his sympathies are.

Peach Blossom Fan is a great historical drama with many typical characters set against an authentic background. The plot is compact, the dialogue brilliantly varied and expressive.

After Hong Sheng and Kong Shangren died, the *zhuan qi* gradually declined and its place in the Chinese theatre was taken by different local operas.

There was a further development in novel-writing during the Qing dynasty. The two great novels written before the opium War are *The Scholars* and *A Dream of Red Mansions.***

Wu Jingzi (1701-1754), the author of *The Scholars*, was a native of Quanjiao in Auhui and came from a family of landowners, many of whom had held official posts. He was a renegade to his class, however, for the whole train of.

儒林外史第一回

說楔子敷陳大義　借名流隱括全文

人生南北多歧路將相神仙也要凡人做百代

興亡朝復蘇江風吹倒前朝樹功名富貴無憑

據費盡心情總把流光誤濁酒三杯沈醉去水

流花謝知何處這一首詞也是個老生常談不

過說人生富貴功名是身外之物但世人一見

了功名便捨著性命去求他及至到手之後味

同嚼蠟自古及今那一個是看得破的雖然如

1803 edition of The Scholars

thought of *The Scholars* is anti-feudal. The author directs his biting satire primarily against the inhuman feudal morality, and secondly against the examination system. The sole aim of those who passed the examinations was to climb the official ladder and make more money; and since they had neither learning nor moral integrity, they could serve only as lackeys of the ruling class. So in Chapter 32, Zang Liaozhai (Tsang Liao-chai) asks Du Shaoqing (Tu Shao-ching) to lend him money to buy a salaried scholar's rank. When Du inquires what use this rank is, he replies that it will enable him to become an official, pass sentence on others and have men beaten. "You ruffian!" cried Du with a laugh. "You are utterly contemptible!" In Chapter 47 again, when the gentry of Wuhe county escort the spirits of deceased relatives to the ancestral temple, in order to ingratiate themselves with the powerful Fang family the members of both the clans of Yu Youda (Yu Yu-ta) and Yu Huaxuan (Yoo Hua-hsuan) follow behind old Mrs. Fang's shrine. In disgust Youda said to Huaxuan, "This district of ours has no morality left!" From his own experience and observation, Wu Jingzi was painfully aware of the hypocrisy and rottenness of feudal society, and he made brilliant use of the novel form to expose them.

The first eighty chapters of *A Dream of Red Mansions* are by Cao Xueqin, the last forty by Gao E. Cao Xueqin was a native of Fengrun in Hebei, whose family served in the Han banner under the Manchus. He was born in Nanking in about 1715 and died in Beijing in 1763. Gao E was a native of Tieling in Liaoning, whose family also served under the Manchus. His dates are uncertain, but he must have written the sequel to *A Dream of Red Mansions* in about 1791.

A Dream of Red Mansions describes a rich, aristocratic family, and is indeed the funeral song of this class. To enjoy a life of luxury, these parasitic landowners put

---

**English translations of both are available. Quotations in the following paragraphs are taken from translations by Yang Hsien-yi and Gladys Yang, published by Foreign Languages Press, 1957 *(Scholars)* and 1978, 1980 *(Dream)*.

Illustration from a 1791 edition of A Dream of Red Mansions

increasing pressure on the peasants on their estates and ruined innocent citizens by contemptible and cruel methods; but in the end they could not escape destruction. The members of the Rong (Jung) and Ning households may present a respectable front to the world, but almost without exception they are selfish, decadent and sadistic, and sometimes they commit open crimes. The excesses of the Jia (Chia) family are summed up by Jiao Da (Chiao Ta) in Chapter 7:

"Little did he [my old master] expect to beget such degenerates, a houseful of rutting dogs and bitches in heat, day in and day out scratching in the ashes** and carrying on with younger brothers-in-law. Don't think you can fool me."

In Chapter 66, someone tells the hero frankly: "The only clean things in that East Mansion of yours are those two stone lions at the gate." And the utter decadence of these aristocrats is revealed by Granny Liu's remark in Chapter 39:

> "Crabs that size cost five silver cents a catty this year . . . . Together with the wine and eatables, that adds up to more than twenty taels of silver. Gracious Buddha! That's enough to keep us country folk for a whole year."

These are realistic descriptions of a landowning family on the eve of the collapse of feudalism. To attack the feudal family system Cao Xueqin created two immortal characters — Jia Baoyu (Chia Pao-yu) and Lin Daiyu (Lin Tai-yu), young rebels who stubbornly oppose old traditions. Baoyu dislikes mixing with the literati and refuses to write *bagu* essays, but enjoys the company of women and sympathizes with the maidservants in his house. Daiyu resembles him. And because the two young people both hate feudal oppression and long for freedom to develop their individuality, a true love springs up between them. As far as these two characters are concerned, Gao E's sequel has nothing significant to add. In the end Daiyu dies of a broken heart and Baoyu runs away, driven to desperation, for young rebels like this could not be tolerated by the forces of reaction. These lovers captured the imagination of readers not only by their tragic romance, but because to a certain extent they reflected the aspirations of the people just before the downfall of feudalism.

For the last century and more this novel has been the most popular work in China.

Other Qing dynasty novels include the anonymous *Lessons for Married Men* and *Flowers in the Mirror* by Li Ruzhen.

**A slang term for adultery between a man and his daughter-in-law.

Last of all we must speak briefly of the local opera.

Local operas, which do not include *za ju* and *zhuan qi*, can be traced back to the Ming dynasty; but they reached full vigour by the eighteenth century. During this period *zhuan qi* were appreciated by a small section of the upper class only, while the great majority of the people enjoyed local opera. The two chief centres were Beijing and Yangzhou.

Though local operas sometimes contain conservative ideas and elements of superstition, in the main they voice what was in the people's minds, their accusations and cries of revolt. Many of them express sympathy for humble folk and hatred for the rich and great; they often give the part of an emperor to a clown, and ruthlessly expose the luxury and savagery of the ruling class.

Most local operas take historical themes. And though the authors are generally unknown they must have included men of genius, for these plays are often magnificently dramatic and have a deep educational significance. Good examples are *The Fisherman's Revenge*, which tells the story of Yuan Xiaoqi, one of the heroes of *Outlaws of the Marsh*, and *The Battle of Wits* describing the Battle of the Red Cliff in the Three Kingdoms period. Sometimes subjects were taken straight from life, as in *Borrowing Boots*, a popular play which ridicules the selfishness and hypocrisy of some townsfolk.

After the Opium War local operas became even more numerous.

During this period, the fifth stage in the development of Chinese literature, poetry and essays were relegated to a secondary position, while fiction and drama came to occupy increasingly important places. The tendentiousness of works of literature became more and more marked.

A Sketch of Daguan Yuan in A Dream of Red Mansions

VI. Literature from the Opium War to the May Fourth Movement

The year between the Opium War of 1840 and the May Fourth Movement of 1919 form the sixth and final stage in the history of classical Chinese literature.

In the latter half of the Qing dynasty, the capitalist countries of the West carried out ceaseless economic and military aggression against China. Thus the feudal society which had lasted for so many centuries collapsed, and China became a semi-feudal, semi-colonial country. At the same time changes took place in class relationships.

All this time the Chinese people continued to fight against aggression and tyranny. The opium War was followed by the Taiping Revolution (1851-1864), the 1898 Reformation, the anti-imperialist Boxer rising (1899-1901), and the 1911 Revolution, to name only the largest revolts. So for the eighty years preceding the May Fourth Movement,the Chinese people persisted in their struggle for democracy. But owing to the weakness of the Chinese bourgeoisie and the lack of working-class leadership, the revolutionaries failed to gain their objective.

Almost without exception, the best writers of this period were sympathetic to the popular cause. The chief poets of these eighty years were Zhang Weiping, Wei Yuan, Zhu Qi and Huang Zunxian. The first three depicted the truth about the First Opium War, revealing the stupidity and cowardice of the government and the courage of the people. Poems like "San Yuan Li" by Zhang Weiping, "Recalling History" by Wei Yuan and "Contemporary Affairs," by Zhu Qi were thoroughly realistic works. Huang Zunxian was an important writer who aspired to start a "revolution in poetry" and founded the "modern" school. Most of the "modern" poems written at that time were somewhat superficial, yet Huang's work is outstanding for its patriotic feeling and close concern with the political and social realities of the time. His language is rich and natural. His poem "Lamenting Pyongyang" records the Chinese defeat at Pyongyang in Korea in 1894, and bitterly reproaches the generals who disgraced China.

> *Of thirty-six strategies, the best is to run:*
> *Horses stampeded, men trampled on each other . . . .*
> *One general was taken captive, one was killed,*
> *And fifteen thousand men laid down their arms.*

"Tonggou" and "Taiwan" were good poems too, fresh and robust compared with the pseudo-classical verse of that time.
In prose the chief writers were Lin Zexu, Zhang Binglin and Liang Qichao. Lin Zexu, the heroic commissioner in Canton who opposed the import of opium, wrote powerful and moving prose on political subjects, including his *Draft Memorandum to the Queen of England* and *Severe Penalties Proposed for Foreign Smugglers*. Zhang Binglin's style is more erudite, but he was a fervent revolutionary who eloquently urged revolt. In his *Declaration on the 240th Anniversary of China's Subjugation by the Manchus*, he wrote:

> Though Greece was conquered, she recovered; and though Poland was dismembered, her people retained their societies. Why should China — our great country with its vast population and fine cultural tradition — prove inferior to these smaller states? Let fathers and sons take counsel together and unite as one; let us wipe our tears and attend this gathering to commemorate the loss

of our independence.

Liang Qichao advocated a new style of prose which had the virtues of simplicity and fluency. Lucid and unhampered by rules, it occasionally used colloquialisms or sentence constructions borrowed from foreign languages. Being clear and expressive it was an effective tool for convincing readers. This is why the writings of Liang Qichao were so popular at the end of the Qing dynasty and the beginning of the republic.

The best-known novelists of this period were Shi Yukun, Liu E, Han Bangqing, Li Baojia, Wu Woyao and Zeng Pu. Li Baojia's two most important works are *Modern Times* and *The Bureaucrats*. He tears the mask from the faces of

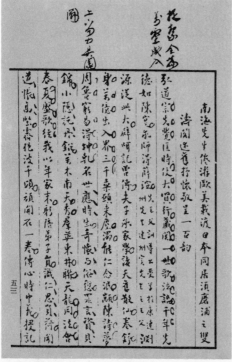

Liang Qichao's manuscript

arrogant foreign missionaries and mandarins who are cowardly bullies. Of Wu Woyao's many novels, the most famous is *Strange Events of the Last Twenty Years*. This attacks not only the bureaucrats but the merchants and scholars too, describing with relish the stupidity of certain "cultured" savants. Zeng Pu is best known for *A Flower in an Ocean of Sin*, a novel about the famous courtesan Golden Flower, which deals with various aspects of society at the end of the Qing dynasty and exposes the corrupt politics and incompetent bureaucracy of that time. In Chapter 5, for instance, we read of a poor official in Beijing, Zhuang Lunqiao, who cannot pay his debts until he wins the emperor's favour and becomes rich. But in Chapter 6, when he is sent to lead China's army and navy against France, he bungles everything.

> He neither knew his officers nor cared for his men, but growing arrogant, arrogated all authority to himself, though all was capable of was tricks and wiles. The French commander did not spare him, however, but catching him off his guard started to bombard his headquarters during a storm. Although Zhuang racked his brains, clever as he was with his pen, he was helpless against cannon; eloquent as he was, he could not withstand the onslaught of the enemy fleet. So he escaped barefoot through the rain, running seven or eight miles without a thought for all the ships and men he was losing, to hide himself inland in a monastery.

This novel, though it was never finished, ranks as one of the best of its time.

During this period, foreign novels translated into Chinese by Lin Shu, Wu Dao and others contributed to the development of Chinese fiction and the Chinese people's understanding of foreign countries.

In drama, while such classical forms as *za ju* and *zhuan qi* were declining, local operas were growing increasingly popular. Carrying on the best traditions of earlier operas like *The Fisherman's Revenge* and *Borrowing Boots*, different localities produced a number of lively plays, often filled with the spirit of revolt or criticism of current abuses. By the time of the 1898 Reformation, Wang Xiaonong had written operas on historical themes to foster patriotism. Thus in *Lamenting at the Ancestral Temple* he describes how when the king of Shu decided to surrender to Wei in A.D. 263, his son Liu Shen killed himself after uttering the following protest:

> *Drums thunder in my ears*
> *As my father approaches General Deng.*
> *I cannot bear to see*
> *A king kneeling before his horse.*
> *Would I could kill all traitors!*
> *Today ends our imperial house;*
> *Fiercely I draw my sword,*
> *Preferring death to dishonour!*

New operas on contemporary themes now became an important part of the Chinese theatre, and played an active role in the political struggle. At this time, too, responding to the political needs of the times, modern plays of the Western type gradually appeared. By the 1911 Revolution there were many repertory companies, among them the Friends' Society, the Spring Sun Society, the Spring Willow Society and the Evolution Club, all of which made their contribution to the Chinese theatre. The plays they produced reflected to a certain extent the popular demand for revolution.

The literature of the period of the democratic revolution also reflected the conflict between the new bourgeois culture and the old feudal one. But since the world had already entered the era of imperialism, the young Chinese capitalist class could not put up a strong fight; thus the bourgeois thinkers of this period showed a striking tendency towards reformism, and the writers did not attain very high standards. Not till the new democratic revolution was inaugurated after the May Fourth Movement was there any marked advance in Chinese literature.

Chronological Table of Chinese Dynasties

Shang Dynasty	c. 16th-11th century B.C.
Western Zhou Dynasty	c. 11th century-771 B.C.
Eastern Zhou Dynasty	770-256 B.C.
Spring and Autumn Period	770-476 B.C.
Warring States Period	475-221 B.C.
Qin Dynasty	221-207 B.C.
Han Dynasty	206 B.C. − A.D. 220
Three Kingdoms Period	A.D. 220-280
Western Jin Dynasty	265-316
Eastern Jin Dynasty	317-420
Southern and Northern Dynasties	420-589
Sui Dynasty	581-618
Tang Dynasty	618-907
Five Dynasties	907-960
Northern Song Dynasty	960-1127
Southern Song Dynasty	1127-1279
Yuan Dynasty	1271-1368
Ming Dynasty	1368-1644
Qing Dynasty	1644-1911
Republic	1912-1949

Index

About the Author

Feng Yuanjun was born in 1900 in Tanghe County, Henan Province. She graduated from the former Women's Normal University in Beijing and obtained the degree of Doctor of Literature at the Sorbonne. After the May Fourth Movement in 1919 she wrote several short stories, among them "Travel" and "Isolation", under the pseudonym "Miss Gan". She had been a lecturer of Beijing University and Beijing Normal University, and professor of Fu Dan University, Wuhan University and Sun Yat-sen University. After the founding of the People's Republic, she was elected deputy to the National People's Congress, member of the Provincial People's Council of Shandong, and vice-chairperson of the Women's Association as well as the Federation of Literary and Art Circles of Shandong. She was also professor, and for a time, vice-president, of the Shandong University. She died in 1974.

Among her writings are *The History of Chinese Poetry*, *A Short History of Chinese Literature*, *On Classical Drama* (all published before 1949), *A Short History of Chinese Literature, Revised* and *A Short History of Classical Chinese Literature*. A collection of her essays on classical literature was published in 1980.